A BRAZILIAN MYSTIC

BEING THE LIFE AND MIRACLES OF
ANTONIO CONSELHEIRO

A
BRAZILIAN MYSTIC

BEING

THE LIFE AND MIRACLES OF
ANTONIO CONSELHEIRO

BY

ROBERT B. CUNNINGHAME GRAHAM

'Adeus, campo, e adeus matto
Adeus, casa onde morei!
Ja' que é forçoso partir
Algum dia te verei!"
Brazilian Rhyme.

BOOKS FOR LIBRARIES PRESS
FREEPORT, NEW YORK

First Published 1920
Reprinted 1971

INTERNATIONAL STANDARD BOOK NUMBER:
0-8369-5623-0

LIBRARY OF CONGRESS CATALOG CARD NUMBER:
70-146856

PRINTED IN THE UNITED STATES OF AMERICA

PREFACE

SOME years ago, when he was President, after having read some tales of mine about the Gauchos, the late Colonel Roosevelt wrote a letter to me. In it he said : " What you and Hudson have done for South America, many have done for our frontiersmen in Texas, Arizona, and New Mexico. Others have written of the Mexican frontiersmen, and written well about them. No one, as far as I know," so he said, " has touched the subject of the frontiersmen of Brazil. Why don't you do it? for you have been there, know them, and speak their lingo. The field is open to you."

I was duly flattered and turned the question over in my mind; then forgot all about it. Things of importance, such as going out to dinner and endeavouring to arrive neither too early nor too late, but just exactly to descend before the door at the right moment —that is to say two or three minutes before eight— came in between the Brazilian frontiersman and my memory, as they are apt to do in civilised society. The years went by, with each one certifying his fellow that had passed, in blameless endeavour, such as that I have described.

Then came the war, and on my passage out to Uruguay, I found myself one morning entering the harbour of Bahia, on the Brazilian coast. The sea was oily; "Portuguese men-of-war" hoisted their fairy little sails, and as the vessel slowed down to half speed, passing the ruinous old fort at the entrance of the bay, backed by a grove of coco-palms looking like ostrich feathers, she put up shoals of flying fish that swept along the surface of the waves, just as a flock of swallows sweep across a field.

The red-roofed city, with its spires and convents, its tall old houses, those in the lower part reaching up almost to the foundations of the houses on the cliff, was unrolled, as it were, in a gigantic cinematograph as the ship steamed into the bay. Eight or ten German vessels were interned and rode at anchor, blistering in the sun. Fleets of the curious catamarans, known as jangadas in Brazil, were making out to sea. Their occupants sat upon a little stool, on the three logs that constitute the embarkation, with feet almost awash, whilst the white-pointed little sails gave the jangadas an air of copying the nautiluses.

Myriads of islands dotted the surface of the vast inlet, the houses on them painted sky-blue and pink or a pale yellow colour. So fair the scene was from the vessel's deck, it seemed that one had come into a land so peaceful that it was quite impossible there could exist in it evil or malice, hatred and envy, or any of the vices or the crimes that curse humanity. One understood the feelings of the apostles when they wished to build their tabernacles ; only the difficulty of finding an Elias or a Moses worth while to build a shanty for, restrained one from incontinently taking up some land and starting in to build.

I stood still gazing, when a voice beside me broke

the spell, bringing me back again to reality, or the illusion of reality that we delude ourselves is life.

"Friend Don Roberto," said the voice, "what things have happened in Bahia! and that not long ago. Scarcely two hundred miles from where we stand took place the rising of Antonio Conselheiro, the last of the Gnostics, who defied all the Brazilian forces for a year or so, and was eventually slain with all his followers. The episode took place not more than five-and-twenty years ago ; you ought to read and then to write about it, for it was made by Providence on purpose for you, and is well fitted to your pen."

I turned and saw my friend Braceras standing by my side, dressed in immaculate white duck. He wore a jipi-japa hat, that must have cost him at the least a hundred dollars. His small and well-arched feet, encased in neat buckskin shoes, showed him a Spaniard of the Spaniards from old Castile, just where it borders on Vizcaya, and the race is purest of the pure. He had the easy manners and the complete immunity from self-preoccupation that makes a man the equal of a king, and just as much at home with fishermen, with cattle-drovers, or any other class of men, as if he were one of them. His hands were nervous, and his blue-black hair was just beginning to turn grey, whilst his dark eyes, his bushy eyebrows, and his closely-shaven face, gave him the look of an ecclesiastic, though not of those whose function is but to say Mass and eat his dinner, as the old adage goes. The name of Conselheiro was known to me but vaguely, although I knew religious movements had been continuous in Brazil since the discovery. I listened to the story, and, when we landed at the capital, bought books about it, bought more in Santos, and as I read and mused upon the tale, the letter from the President came back into my mind.

The events all happened in the wild region known as the Sertão,* lying between the States of Pernambuco and Bahia, unknown, I take it, geographically, to ninety-nine per cent. of educated men.

The followers of Antonio Conselheiro were, almost to a man, what are known as Jagunços, a term invented for the most prominent of the cattle men who live in the Sertão, and signifying something between a bully and a fighting-cock, and by degrees applied to all of them, as the term Gaucho is in Argentina, Guaso in Chile, and Llanero in the vast, grassy plains upon the Orinoco, to the same class of man. 'Tis true they did not live upon a frontier, except the ever-shifting barrier between the old world and the new, or that which just as constantly is changing its position and its course, betwixt our modern life and medievalism. Still, these are frontiers just as well marked indeed as those that arbitrarily separate two countries—in fact, are really better far defined. As I read on about the semi-Gnostic and his adventures of the spirit, and the adventurous lives his followers led, although they too, or most of them, were deeply tinged with either superstition or religion—for who shall say where the one ends and his twin brother starts?—I felt Braceras

---

* Sertão may be translated "highlands," though that does not entirely give the sense of the word, which infers what we call "back-lying" in Scotland. It is a high plateau, covered with scrub.
  The mark over the "a," called "til" in Portuguese, gives a nasal sound, almost as if the word were written "Sertawn."

had been right in what he said about the subject, and
of the interest it contained.

The life in the material sense was simple : but in its
background there was evidence of faith of a peculiar
kind, tinged with fanaticism. Their faith, as often
happens, but little influenced their daily lives, which
were passed in the open air on horseback, herding
their cattle, dressed in their deerskin clothes.

As I wrote of it, looking at the drops of moisture
coursing down the window-panes (for it was autumn
in the north when I began to write), I used to wonder
if the sun was shining in Brazil, as I remembered it,
for I could see the sodden stooks of corn out in the
fields, with the rain falling on them, and on the ships
in the strait, fairway channel as they crept up and
down the Clyde.

Although Antonio Conselheiro had paid the
penalty of his credulity or faith, I felt the wild
life in the Sertão was going on as usual, and the
vaqueiros were galloping about, with their long, iron-
shod cattle-goads sloped forward, just as of old the
men of Annandale carried their rusty spears.

I fancied I could see them land upon their feet like
cats, when a horse fell with them, just as once, long ago
in Entre Rios, I saw a man fall suddenly and come
off running, unharmed, although his horse had its
neck dislocated. A pity, too, because the horse, a
little " gateado," if I remember rightly, was one that
you could turn upon a hide in Gaucho phrase; and
for the man—your damned bronchitis took him off,
and he died slovenly, within a month or two.

This kind of book is bound to find its way, and

shortly, to an old bookstall, there to be sold with other bargains for a penny, after the fashion of the sparrows in the Holy Scriptures, for it treats of unfamiliar people and of a life unknown and unsuspected by the general. It is no matter, for he who writes a book writes for his own peculiar pleasure, and if he does not, he had better far abstain from writing, for that which pleases not the writer of the work can scarce please anybody.

If it is fated that my account of the Jagunço mystic should lie rotting in the rain upon a stall, so be it, for so it was decreed; though it were better fitting it should cockle in the sun and shrivel up, just as a dead body shrivels up in the dry air of the Sertão.

Shrivel or rot, it is all one to me. Just as the struggle is the thing worth struggling for and the result a secondary affair, so is the writing of a book what matters to the writer of it, for he has had his fight.

If it but please himself he has his public and his reward assured, in regions where the rain cannot offend him, and where the fiercest sun that ever blazed upon the sand is tempered pleasantly.

R. B. CUNNINGHAME GRAHAM.

Ardoch, 1919.

A BRAZILIAN MYSTIC

BEING THE LIFE AND MIRACLES OF
ANTONIO CONSELHEIRO

INTRODUCTION

WHAT is called the Sertão* of the Brazilian provinces of Pernambuco and Bahia is one of the most curious regions of South America. It is also one of the least known to the outside world.

Life goes on there much as it has gone on for the last three hundred years. The people mostly are engaged in cattle farming, and live on horseback. They dress in leather, on account of the dense scrub; their daily lives are hard and perilous; religion occupies a chief place in their minds.

The two provinces of Bahia and Pernambuco meet in the vague region of the Sertão, an elevated plateau between two thousand and three thousand feet in height, backed by more or less pronounced ranges of mountains or of hills, whose distance from the coast rarely exceeds two hundred or two hundred and fifty miles. This plateau has a climate and a flora of its own, the former ranging from great extremes of heat to a considerable degree of cold, taking into consideration the latitude in which it lies.

* Sertão is a word hardly possible to translate except by a periphrasis. It means " wooded, back-lying highlands."

The flora chiefly consists of thorny trees and plants, known in Brazil as " caatinga," a Tupi word signifying " bush or scrub."

The country gradually rises from the coast to the plateau of the Sertão, and the climate, vegetation, and soil of it are all widely different from those of the littoral districts.

All these conditions, together with the isolation in which they have lived for three hundred years, have left their impress on the population, making them a race apart—a race of centaurs, deeply imbued with fanaticism, strong, honest, revengeful, primitive, and refractory to modern ideas and life to an extraordinary degree. Their existence centres, and has always done so, round their cattle, for the Sertão is little fitted for most kinds of agriculture. The arid nature of the soil, the long-continued droughts, the extraordinary difference of the temperature between the day and night, all tend to make the Sertanejos (*i.e.*, the inhabitants of the Sertão) a people set apart from all the world. Their ancestors, when they left Portugal, had just emerged from their long contest with the Moors. To them, religion was not a faith only, but a mark of race—a rallying-point, a war-cry, and a bond uniting them to one another, in a way difficult for modern men to understand. With us religion is a personal thing ; we take it, according to our individual temperament, in many differing ways. Some, not the highest minds, look on it as a sort of mumbojumbo whereby to save their souls. Others, again, regard it as a means whereby life is ennobled, death's terrors exorcised, and the world improved.

The Portuguese, when they set out to colonise Brazil, I fancy, looked at religion chiefly from the point of view of nationality. If you were a true Portuguese, white on all four sides, as ran the saying, you were a Christian. You could not be otherwise, for Jews and Moors and other infidel were all the enemies, both of the true faith and of your native land. Although the Portuguese held the same iron faith as did the Spaniards of those times, yet in their nature there was a vein of almost northern mysticism—a belief in fairies, spirits of the night and of the mountain, a fear of werwolves, and a sort of sentimentalism, especially to be observed in the two northern provinces, in which the Celtic strain of blood was most predominant. Thus were the people, both by descent and by their isolated life, especially susceptible to wild religious creeds, and were, in fact, in point of faith, mental equipment, and religious temperament, not very much unlike some of the Gnostic sects in Asia Minor in the first and second centuries. In the fashion of the Gnostic sects, the people of the Sertão looked to no central authority. Their parish priest, to them, was Pope, Council, and Father of the Church. There might be greater, or as great, authorities in what they called " as terras grandes" (i.e., the great or foreign lands); but they looked on them just as one looks on death, as something terrible and vague, although not imminent.

These kind of folk, so to speak, culminated in the State of Bahia, for it is there that they have always manifested their most peculiar traits. The territory is immense, bounded on the north by the province of Sergipe del Rey and Pernambuco, on the south by Porto Seguro and Minas Geraes, on the west by Pernambuco, from which the Rio São Francisco separates it, and on the east by the Atlantic Ocean.   It lies entirely in the tropics, from 10° to 16° south latitude, and is about three hundred and fifty miles in length by about two hundred and forty broad.

Such a vast extent of territory has given room for the inhabitants of the Sertão to form a world entirely of their own.

Brazil, at the time of the conquest, was divided into captaincies (*capitanias*), great tracts of land having been given to men styled " donatories."   The first event in the history of the State of Bahia is the shipwreck of Diogo Alvarez Correa, a man destined to play a curious rôle in the new land to which his ship was bound.   No certainty exists as to the date, except a passage in Herrera, one of the historians of the Indies, in which he says, speaking of the shipwreck of two Spanish vessels that left San Lucar de Barraméda, in September, 1534, and were wrecked on the Brazilian coast in 1635 : " Here they found a Portuguese who said that there were five-and-twenty years he had been amongst the Indians."*

This Portuguese, one Diogo Alvarez Correa, had by the time that he was found, after his long residence amongst the Indians, become a man of note.   His name amongst them was Caramarú, which is interpreted " the man of fire "— a title that he had acquired by having brought a gun ashore with him.

---

* " Onde hallaron un Portuguez que dixo que avia veyente y cinco años que estaua entre los Indios."

Henderson, in his " History of Brazil,"* says that in his time (1821) a man still living at Port Seguro had in his possession an old manuscript which affirms that Gaspar de Lemos, one of the first discoverers of Brazil, upon a voyage back to Portugal, entered the River Ilheos, near Bahia, landed, and was suddenly attacked by Indians. Correa, one of his crew, had no time to re-embark, and thus remained amongst the savages. As he had married many times and oft, amongst the Indians, and spoke their language, he was a valuable man to find.

In the wrecked Spanish vessel came the first donatory, one Francisco Peyreya Coutinho, a personage of rank. Coutinho was a Portuguese fidalgo†— i.e., a nobleman who had but recently returned from India, where he had served with honour and rendered important services to the State. The King, Don John III., having divided all Brazil into capitanias, granted Coutinho all the country lying between the point of Padrao, now known as San Antonio and the River San Francisco, together with the Reconcava of Bahia—i.e., the greater part of the extensive bay.

This gentleman fitted out his expedition after the fashion of the times. As his first action was, after having run up a stockade, to build a church, quite evidently he understood the full force of the proverb, " Pray to God, but strike home with the mace."‡ His expedition comprised a chaplain, what in those days were known as reformed—i.e., retired—soldiers, and

* Henderson, " History of Brazil," London, 1821, p. 310.
† Fidalgo—literally " a son of somebody, or of something."
‡ Á Dios rogando, y con la maza dando.

many men of wealth.   Brazil being a tropical country, and the Portuguese never having held the Spanish views upon the ignominy of commerce, and being less set on finding gold mines, and on the whole far less ferocious in their desire to save the souls of the poor Indians, nearly all the donatories embarked in sugar planting.   Coutinho did the same, and all seemed flourishing for several years.   They built a chapel on the site, where now stands the hermitage of Our Lady of the Victories.

Negroes were unprocurable, as the slave trade in Brazil only began in 1574.

The climate made field labour for white men almost impossible, although the Portuguese did not look down upon all manual toil, after the Spanish way. Still, labour was essential for their sugar fields, so they began to make the Indians slaves.   No race of men in all the world was less inclined to sit down quietly in a slavish state than were the Indians of Brazil.   Thus war was certain from the first, though the first settlers never understood the race.   One thing is to the credit of the Portuguese : they seem to have made no pretence about the glory of the Lord as did the Spaniards, in like circumstances.   So when they made a man a slave they did not trouble overmuch about his soul.

Still, they were not entirely free from the ideas that influenced their age, and always took a good store of priests and friars with them to all their conquests— perhaps as a precaution, or perhaps from habit, or because it was enjoined upon them by their Government.   In all the conquests of Brazil the Jesuits took a considerable share.

Vincente Moreira, Treasurer to Our Lord the King of Portugal, in a report he makes to Mem de Sá, Governor of Brazil, laments that a chief of the Indians, whom he calls Wry-Mouth (*Boca Torta*), refused to give up eating human flesh, so that the Government was forced to march against him and burn his village, and after burning it, and killing many of the enemy, ordered the Jesuit father to build a church wherein mass could be said, the doctrine taught, with reading, writing, and other good customs."*

Still, the Portuguese seem to have kept their punitive expeditions, as we should call them nowadays, and their endeavours to introduce " good customs and a knowledge of their faith, apart from one another. We never read, in Brazil at least, of a single instance of a conqueror who, as Cortes in Mexico, was even more eager than the priests to bring the Indian flock into the fold. The usual treatment of the natives by Coutinho and his followers was bound to bring the usual results. The Indians broke into revolt. Most of the territory now comprised in the State of Bahia was at that time inhabited by a tribe of Indians called Tupinambás,† a fierce and war-like tribe. They spread at one time over nearly all the coastal districts of Brazil. Their language was nearly allied to Guarani, as spoken by the Paraguayans to-day.‡ Their

* " E leer e escrever e outras boas costumes."—Vincente Monteiro Tezoureiro del Rey Nosso senhor, in a report to Mem de Sa, Governor of Brazil, in the " Documentos relativos a Mem de Sa," published in the " Annaes da Bibliotheca Nacional, do Rio de Janeiro," vol. xxvii., p. 194.

† These Indians were a branch of the great Tupi race.

‡ Guarani and Tupi are closely allied tongues, and in general nearly all the place-names in that vast territory are in these languages.

place-names are almost identical. Anyone with a smattering of Guarani can make out most of the place-names in the province of Bahia, apart from those in Portuguese, given by the conquerors. The Tupi-nambás seem to have been fiercer and more warlike than the Guaranís of Paraguay. Above all things, they were hardy and enduring to an extraordinary degree. These qualities they have transmitted to the Sertanejos of Bahia, most of whom have a tinge of Indian blood. The Tupinambás, or, to be accurate, the Tupiniquin Indians, most probably a branch of the more well-known tribe, soon grew sick of continued work; and the very probable injustices they had to suffer at the hands of Coutinho and his colonists, especially, we may suppose, the forced introduction of "good customs," always so disagreeable both to the Indian and the white man alike, drove them into revolt. They carried on for six or seven years a long-drawn-out warfare with the intruders on their lands.

This warfare had all the well-known characteristics of colonial wars. The Indians attacked by night, and burned the sugar factories. They cut off small bodies of the Portuguese, whom they surprised. No doubt, now and then, they massacred the settlers; at any rate, they made the colony untenable. Coutinho had to

---

Early in the history of Brazil, and perhaps even before the conquest, Tupi became the general means of communication. It is now much mixed with Portuguese—for instance, as to numerals, for the Tupis only counted up to five.

It is "A Lingoa Geral" (the General Language), and it is supposed was so used by the varying tribes from remote ages. It runs from the southern part of the Orinoco to Paraguay and the Argentine province of Corrientes.

re-embark with all his men, taking with him Correa as interpreter. Driven ashore by a violent gale, not far from the entrance to the harbour of Bahia, they were attacked, slaughtered and eaten, for the tribe into whose hands they fell were cannibals. Correa-Caramarú escaped, owing to his knowledge of the Indian tongue.

Eventually, by way of matrimony, often continued and well thought out, we may suppose, as regards the rank and circumstances of his brides' families, he became a prince. His offspring, the Jesuit Vascon-cellos,* who wrote his life, informs us, were numerous, and it is said that many families of Bahia still trace their ancestry to the " man with the gun."

Caramarú—Correa's head wife, the daughter of an Indian chief, baptised as Donna Catharina—sleeps in the suburb of Victoria, in the Church of Our Lady of Grace. She accompanied her husband to Europe, where he must have been as much at sea after so many years of Indian life as she was herself. Her baptism took place in Paris. At it she relinquished her Indian name of Paraguassu, and took that of the Queen of France.

This Indian lady, worthy to be placed beside Pocahontas in the roll of fame, has the following epitaph upon her tomb: " This is the sepulchre† of Donna Catharina Alvarez, Lady of this Captaincy of

---

* This author did not write till one hundred and fifty years after Caramarú's death, but I see no reason to doubt his word or his facts.

† "Sepultura de Dona Catharina Alvarez, Senhora desta Capitania da Bahia, a qual ella, a seu marido Diogo Alvarez Correa, natural de Vianna, deram uos Senhores Reys de Portugal, fez, e deu esta Capella ao Patriarca St. Bento, Anno de 1582."

Bahia, which she and her husband, Diogo Alvarez
Correa, a native of Vianna, gave to the Kings of Por-
tugal, and built and gave this chapel to the Patriarch
St. Bento, in the year 1582."

None of Correa's other wives left epitaphs.

He himself lived to a ripe old age, and in the year
1549 he welcomed Thomé de Sousa, the new Captain-
General, and lodged him and his followers in his
village, whilst a new settlement, now the City of
Bahia, was being built.

Donna Catharina's Indian name, Paraguassú, is that
of the river near which she was born. Her husband's
birthplace is a delightful little town in Portugal, in
the province of the Minho, not very far from Spain.
It stands, the houses clustering round the beautiful,
flamboyant Igreja Matriz, a mine of old-world and
arcaded streets, all paved with cobble stones. The
River Lima, which the Roman soldiers took for
Lethe, washes its walls.*   Although Correa had
drunk its waters in his childhood, he found those of
the Paraguassú more potent, and laid his bones far
from the river of his youth.

Diogo Correa-Caramarú and Paraguassú-Catharina
were thus the originators of the race that was to have
so large a share in the destiny, not only of Bahia, but
of all Brazil. The Indians that the Portuguese found
living upon the land were no less hardy and warlike
than themselves.

---

* Lucius Junius Brutus had to plunge into it, carrying his standard,
to induce his soldiers to cross it.   The poet Diogo Bernardes says:

" Junto do Lima, claro e fresco rio
Que Lethe se chamou antiguamente."

The first cross—*i.e.*, the cross between the white and Indian—is known throughout Brazil as a " Mestiço," —*i.e.*, a half-breed. The introduction of the negro brought another cross and opened the way to a bewildering number of half and quarter breeds between the different races of Indians, negroes, and the whites.

These in Brazil go under many names, not very easy to keep apart and to distinguish by the foreigner. Though the colours blend into one another, the infinite variety of gradations tends to bring about one or two separate types. As a general rule, it may be said that the Mulatto, the cross between the negro and the white, presents a type of man, strong, bulky, and robust, but indolent and unprogressive, with a strong tendency to religious fervour. This type is generally to be found in the coast districts and rarely penetrates to the Sertão.

The Mamaluco, called also Curiboca, is the half-breed between the white and Indian.

Lastly, the Cafuz is the result of interbreeding between the negro and the Indian, generally the Indian of the Tupi race.

The names of Curiboca and Mamaluco are of Indian origin, and are derived from Tupi words : in the first instance, " Curiboc " (*i.e.*, proceeding from the white), and in the second, " Mamaluco," from " mama " to mix and " rucca " to draw. All these strange names are further complicated by the term "Caboclo," generally used of Indians who have attained to some degree of civilisation, but often merely to designate a rustic, country fellow.

All these three divisions have bred and interbred,

and keep on doing so ; but in the long run the white blood generally prevails.   The Mamaluco and Cafuz are seldom seen upon the coast, and it is from their ranks that the interior has been chiefly populated. Just as the Mulatto usually is gay and temperamental, so is the Curiboca almost always taciturn, fanatical in his religious beliefs, steadfast in all his doings, a cruel enemy, and an equally stanch friend.

Though not so powerful in a single effort as the Mulatto, he is incredibly enduring of all kinds of hardships.   His frame is light and active, his beard sparse, his speech slow and measured, and he is not without traces of ferocity, even of cruelty in his composition, inherited with his Indian blood.

The Cafuz, known in the Spanish republics as the Zambo, is the lowest of the three types.   Not lacking in physical strength or energy, his mental outlook is not infrequently backward and savage, and his features often squat and simian-looking.   Roughly, it may be said that all three types afford a better field for the religious enthusiast or agitator to work upon than any to be met with throughout America.   The agitation or enthusiasm, however, never exceeds the limits of the Catholic Church, and all the jarring sects, so common in the United States, are quite unknown in any portion of Brazil.

Such movements as have arisen in Brazil—and they have been extremely numerous—have always been what one may style revolutions of the interior grace, to use a theological term, rather than of forms of Church government or of the right of individual interpretation of the Scriptures, such as have generally given rise to the myriad sects amongst the English and Americans. As the repeated crossings and intercrossings of the three races have produced a type of man, neither all Indian nor all white, but with a certain strain of negro blood who has become the inhabitant of the Sertoes,* slight, active, olive-coloured, and with abundant hair and scanty beard, so have they formed a type of mind highly receptive of religious mania.

Towards the production of this physical and moral type, undoubtedly the strange nature of the country, known as the Sertão, has powerfully contributed, as also has the isolation of their lives. From the earliest colonial times the crown of Portugal neglected the Sertão because its only industry was cattle-breeding, and this did not afford in those days a good field for taxation, which chiefly fell upon the gold mines of Goyáz.

This circumstance, although in some respects it probably contributed to the increase of cattle-breeding, still further shut off the inhabitants from communion with the outer world.

" To-day," as João Ribeira says in his " History of Brazil,"† " the Sertanejo presents a type finer and purer than the dweller on the coast, where the race is so much mixed with the negro blood.

" The Sertanejos are dark-skinned indeed, but their hair is often fair. . . . Being accustomed from their earliest youth to the use of arms, they are apt to fly to them unduly to revenge even the smallest slight. . . . They are suspicious of all outside influence, and refractory to modern life."

* Plural of Sertão.
† João Ribeira, " Historio do Brazil," Rio de Janeiro, 1909.

In point of fact it took eighty to one hundred years to open up the Sertão properly. Only in 1715, and after the Treaty of Madrid was signed between Spain and Portugal, was the whole country free for cattle men to settle in and to possess. At first they settled timidly upon the foothills, then gradually passed them and spread to the interior ; but the chief road of Brazilian exploration and of settlement was by the River San Francisco, the only river of considerable size upon that region of the coast. They advanced along it, settling both sides, and by degrees came to the falls of Paulo Affonso, which checked their progress, making them spread out towards the interior. These falls, whose very name is generally unknown to those who have not visited Brazil, are a worthy rival of Niagara. Their height is somewhere about two hundred and fifty feet, their volume little inferior to Niagara, but their surroundings, and the fact that just below the falls the river is narrowed to a chasm between two lofty rocks, makes them superior in interest to the more famous falls. The tropic vegetation, with the groves of palms and of bamboos fringing the bank, the brightly coloured birds, the solitude, the perpetual rainbow that hangs upon the columns of white spray resembling a fog-bow seen at sea, and the deep channels just below the rocks cut into rapids and a thousand cataracts, make the Brazilian waterfall one of the finest in the world. Thus, in the Sertão all has contributed to a type of man and to a scheme of life perhaps unique in a world where all types tend to disappear. In fact, in all Brazil the Sertão alone has the traditions of a national life, and it is there that one must look for the Brazilian with all his virtues and his vices most accentuated.

Lying as the district does within the tropics, in latitude 13° below the line, the rains should be abundant and the climate tropical,* as they are upon the coast. It is far different in the Sertão. As the road nears the mountains, little by little both soil and vegetation change. The black, rich earth of the low alluvial plains melts by degrees and loses colour, until a region of a red, friable, sandy soil appears. That is the characteristic colour of the soil of the Sertão, and also of great tracts of country in the interior of Brazil. The giants of the primeval forest, with their dark, metallic leaves all twisted round with rope-like creeping plants, whose branches of bright scarlet or vivid yellow blossoms hang in festoons, or, reaching up above the stem, appear to be the flowers of the tree to which they cling, disappear by degrees. Their place is taken by the cactuses and the Bromeliaceæ, especially the variety called in Brazil Caraguatá, and in Jamaica the wild pineapple. Ceibas and Jacarandás, Sapucayas, Jequitibas, Mocahybas, and all the myriad trees that flower and die unknown in the great forests of the coast, all disappear. The scrubby, thorny palm of the Sertão, called Yatai in Paraguay, the Mangabeira, with its whitish-yellow flowers that look like jasmine, and the Imbuzeiro, whose leaves resist the devouring droughts of summer

---

* As in most tropical countries, there are only two seasons, the wet and dry. In the Sertão they are known as " Verde e Magrem " —literally, the " green and fasting."

and furnish fodder for the cattle, and a dish known
to the Sertanejos as "imbuzada," made from a paste
procured by pounding up the nuts, alone endure the
climate and the scant, sandy soil.

These and a thorny scrub are the chief vegetation
of the "caatingas" as they are called, those little open
plains bounded by thick, almost impenetrable bush,
which tears all clothing but the deerskin that the
Vaqueiros* wear.   Lichens and moss all disappear in
the dry, arid climate, whilst here and there under
a palm-tree are seen those water holes known as
"cacimbas," which the inhabitants, who wage a constant war with thirst at certain seasons of the year, dig
where a trace of vegetation shows there is water
underneath the ground.   Little by little the landscape
grows impassive, almost menacing, naked, inhospitable,
and monotonous.   It is a land of thirst, of great
extremes of temperature, of sudden storms, of frozen
nights succeeding days of the intensest heat ; a land
where man has got to fight for his existence against
drought, storms, heat, cold, hunger, and thirst, and
thus becomes toughened and hardened, bodily and
mentally thrown back upon himself, fanatical in
his religion, introspective, visionary, brave, hospitable,
suspicious, cruel and generous, made up of contradic-
tions, fitted to struggle with the daily trials of his life.
In the blazing heat and scorching cold the very
plants get stunted ; the leguminosæ that generally
grow so tall within the tropics, here are dwarfed.
Amongst that family, the plants called "as favellas"
by the Sertanejos, unclassified as far as at present

* Vaqueiro = cattle-herder.

known in any catalogue of plants, has the strange property that one side of its leaf retains the coldness of the night air, at the same time the other keeps the noonday temperature. Other plants, such as that known as " as patatas do Vaqueiro,"* have roots that penetrate yards under the surface of the ground. It also furnishes a tuber not unlike the potato, which in the droughts often is the sole food of the inhabitants.

This struggle for existence amongst plants and trees presents its counterpart amongst mankind. The climate sees to it that only those most fitted to resist it arrive at manhood, and the rude life they subsequently lead has forged a race as hard as the Castilians, the Turk, the Scythians of old, or as the Mexicans.

No race in all America is better fitted to cope with the wilderness. The Sertanejo is emphatically what the French call " a male." His Indian blood has given him endurance and a superhuman patience in adversity. From his white forefathers he has derived intelligence, the love of individual as opposed to general freedom inherent in the Latin races, good manners, and a sound dose of self-respect. His tinge of negro blood, although in the Sertão it tends to disappear out of the race, at least in outward characteristics, may perchance have given him whatever qualities the African can claim. Far from demonstrative, he yet feels deeply ; never forgets a benefit, and cherishes an insult as if it were a pearl of price, safe to revenge it when the season offers or when the enemy is off his guard.

* The plant is described, but not classified, in Henderson's
" Brazil." It is probably of the Convolvulus family.

Centaurs before the Lord, the Sertanejos do not appear (almost alone of horsemen) to have that pride in their appearance so noticeable in the Gaucho, the Mexican, and in the Arabs of North Africa. Seated in his short curved saddle, a modification of the "recao" used on the Pampas of the Argentine, the Sertanejo lounges, sticks his feet forward, and rides, as goes the saying, all about his horse, using, of course, a single rein, and the high hand all natural horsemen affect.* Yet, when a bunch of cattle break into a wild stampede, the man is suddenly transformed. Then he sits upright as a lance, or, bending low over his horse's neck, flies at a break-neck pace, dashing through the thick scrub of the Caatingas in a way that must be seen to be believed. Menacing boughs hang low and threaten him. He throws himself flat on the horse's back, and passes under them. A tree stands in his way right in the middle of his headlong career. If his horse, highly trained and bitted, fails to stop in time, he slips off like a drop of water from a pane of glass at the last moment, or if there is the smallest chance of passing on one side, lies low along his horse's flank after the fashion of an old-time Apache or Comanche on the war-path.

The frightened cattle rush through the Caatinga with the speed of thought. The thick scrub opens at their passage, and hides them utterly. The Sertanejo follows, and he too passes and is swallowed up, leaving no trace of where he has passed through.

* The bit used all over Brazil is a modification of the bit brought by the conquerors, and is not unlike that of the horse in King Charles's statue in Trafalgar Square.

"Where the steer* passes, there the Vaqueiro with his horse can pass," is a proverbial saying in the Sertão, and it is certainly a fact. If the bunch of cattle that he is pursuing should be sufficiently incautious to leave the shelter of the woods and enter one of the little plains that stretch like lakes or like oases in the middle of the woods, the Vaqueiro, brandishing his long and iron-tipped goad, called a "guiada," is on their flanks within the twinkling of an eye, and turns them back into the road for home. As a general rule unless frightened by fire or when they run before a storm, cattle—that is, semi-domesticated cattle—settle down when they are turned. It takes a good horse and a bold rider to come up with a bunch of frightened cattle upon any ground; but then no horseman in the world can hold his own with the Vaqueiro of the Sertão dressed in his panoply† of leather and on the ground he knows.

* "Por onde passa o boi, passa o vaqueiro com o seu caballo."

† I use the word "panoply" advisedly, for the effect of the stiff leather clothes is very like that of armour. The outfit consists of : The hat (chapeio) ; this is low, very stiff-brimmed, and not much unlike the steel hat our troops use in France ; it is kept in place by a leather chin-strap. The leather gauntlets ("as luvas"). The skin-tight trousers ("as perneras") ; they have to be tight-fitting, for any fold would catch the thorns and tear in their wild gallops through the bush. The jacket, called "o gibão," which literally means a doublet. The knee-caps ("as joelheiras"), to protect the knees from thorns, and stiff gaiters, known as "guarda-pes," complete the accoutrement. The horse, too, has his armour, without which he would be torn to pieces in the thorns. Over his quarters falls a covering of hide which reaches almost to his hocks. His "joelheiras" protect his knees as they do those of the Vaqueiro who directs him. Lastly, "o peitoral" covers his shoulders and protects the chest. The horse is seldom shod, but does not seem to feel the want of shoes even amongst the stones. The horses of the Sertão are small, never exceeding fourteen hands. They all are trained to

When once the Vaqueiro sees the cattle begin to settle down and " string out," as it is called, in a long file, or stand and gaze and then begin to eat, he raises the curious chant called O Aboio—that is the Cattle Song. Sometimes it is sounded with a horn ; but on occasions such as this the Boiaro* begins to sing in a low, melancholy voice. The effect is soothing on the cattle, and the drawn-out syllables—

> " E cou mansão
> E cou e cão "—

have a strange effect as they go echoing through the woods. All this occurs if the stampeded cattle keep together and are able to be turned. If, on the other hand, a beast or two cut from the herd and take their course alone, the Vaqueiro, who cannot use the lazo on account of the thick scrub, resorts to the " saiada," which generally succeeds in taming even the wildest beast.

Keeping his horse in hand and watching well his opportunity, the Vaqueiro, when he sees an open place, loosens his head and spurs him. In a bound or two he puts himself close alongside the steer. Then, bending in the saddle, he takes a firm hold of the bullock's tail, and turns his horse a little outwards, and with a powerful twist and jerk, he throws the animal upon its side.† The shock is violent, and the

---

amble, and are descended from the horses brought by the conquerors, without any admixture of blood, since the conquest.

   * There is no word I know in English to express Boiaro. There may have been one in Sussex, where oxen were used for ploughing and in carts. The French " bouvier " is an exact translation.

   † Sometimes this feat is performed with the goad, which is pressed on the animal's thigh as the hind feet leave the ground.

feat not easy to perform. Quicker than thought, before the animal can rise, the Vaqueiro springs from his horse, alighting like a cat upon his feet. His horse stands still, trained to avoid the long hide reins which the Vaqueiro throws upon the ground. Then, rushing to the prostrate animal, he drags its forefoot over the near horn and leaves it helpless on the ground. His horse awaits him like a statue, and he, bounding upon its back, is off again after another animal. The whole thing passes in a flash, and in an instant the scrub has closed upon the horseman, leaving the bullock till he comes back again to take its foot down from its horn.

This operation is a dangerous one, for by this time the animal has got its wind again, and not unlikely charges the instant that it feels that it is free. Then comes the use of the long open reins, which generally are seven feet in length. Holding them by their extremities, the Vaqueiro carefully goes up to the fallen animal, taking good care to keep a tight hand on his reins.

Sometimes the shock has taken all the fight out of the bullock, who rises sullenly and then begins to eat. In that case he gives no more trouble, and can be driven peaceably towards the bunch of cattle which by that time is being kept together by several horsemen. At other times he charges savagely. Then the Vaqueiro either mounts as quickly as he can and gallops off, or, diving underneath his horse, mounts on the offside, leaving the bullock looking for him in amazement. This sort of life, sustained upon a diet of dried beef, called by the Vaqueiros Carne do

vento* (that is, wind-dried meat), and Angú, a sort of
porridge made of maize or from a paste of the nuts
of the palm called Coco Naia, makes a race of men
not to be daunted even by the climate of the Sertão.

On foot they walk like sailors just come ashore
after a whaling cruise, rolling about upon their legs,
bandied by early riding, as do the cow-punchers of
Western America, and as the Medes were said to walk
by the Greek historians.

Nevertheless, they go out with a forked stick and
a long knife on foot to kill the jaguar,† called by them
Suçuarana, which must be a Tupi or some other
Indian word.   The method they adopt is simple, for
having tracked the jaguar, they rouse him from his
lair with dogs, and when he charges, as he generally
does when he finds himself at bay, the man who
carries the forked stick drops on one knee and catches
the beast with it as he springs.   His companion, who
either has a long, sharp knife or a short, heavy spear,
loses no time in burying it in the jaguar's belly or his
throat.   This sport, which must be quite as exciting

* Carne do vento is the Charqui of the Argentines, the Tasajo of
the Mexicans, or the Biltong of the Boers.   It is made by cutting
beef into long thin strips and exposing it to the sun for about three
days.   It can be dipped in orange, lemon, or other juices to give
it a flavour.   Few European teeth stand it long.   Pounded and
mixed with a little cinnamon it is life-sustaining on a journey, but
scarcely palatable.   The Sertanejos do not use it in this manner as
far as I know, but they do use a curious confection known as " esteira
de Imbu," which is the juice of the Imbuzeiro run into a mould and
hardened.   It is then rolled into thin cylinders like wafers.   It keeps
a long time, is very handy for a journey, and very sustaining.

† Jaguar means dog in Guarani, and a tiger is called Jaguareté—
that is, the big dog ; for the Guaranis did not know the cat till after
the conquest.   The first cats taken to Asuncion sold for a pound of
gold.   When I knew the place the price had fallen.

as shooting pigeons from a trap, is often fatal to the sportsmen if anything goes wrong. In Brazil, in Mexico and Venezuela, many large cattle farms have a man called a tigrero, for the jaguar is generally called el tigre (the tiger) in the Spanish Republics, whose office is to kill the tigers who prey upon the stock.

The fight with the droughts, which are the curse of the Sertão, and the isolated life probably account for the intensity of the religious faith of the inhabitants. Abandoned as they have been for the last three hundred years, with scarcely any intercourse with anybody from the outside world, Catholicism with them has taken on many of the characteristics of the hardest Presbyterianism. Sermons are filled with hell and with its flames. The pains and penalties that await the sinner, the tortures of the damned, are all set forth with just as faithful ministration as used to be the fashion of the Cameronians of old.

Their religion neither consoles nor softens. A fitting faith for a hard land, it has produced a people hard as itself. Faithful indeed to the shedding of blood, their own or that of others, they look up to their priests, or to the various religious leaders who have from time to time arisen amongst them, as something superhuman and in direct communication with the Deity.

Nature and circumstances seem to have worked together to prepare the inhabitants of the Sertão for the great adventure into which they plunged in 1896.

The history of the numberless religious communities in Brazil—for they can hardly be termed "sects," never having left the Church in which they took their origin—is highly curious, and hitherto has not been dealt with adequately. Yet they have been continuous, and now and then fraught with considerable danger to the State. It affords field for speculation why the Portuguese, so much less fanatical upon the whole than were the Spaniards in the New World, should have exhibited such strange religious movements in Brazil, and more especially in the State of Bahia, almost the first of the territories to be colonised.

The reason may be found perhaps in the clash or temperaments involved in the excessive crossing of the various types. The Portuguese, a race of Latin stock, mixed in the north with Celtic and in the south with Arab and with Berber blood, had, at the time the conquest of Brazil was carried out, become infected, in Lisbon and the surrounding district, with a strain of negro blood. It was estimated that there were at least ten thousand negroes in the capital, the result of the Portuguese conquests on the Guinea coasts.

Garcia de Rezende, a writer of those days (1530), says in verse, of which the following is the free rendering : " We see the number of slaves put into the kingdom increase so much that the natives will have to go. Thus, soon, they [the captives] will number more than us, as I see the question."*

Thus the Portuguese at that time, or at least those coming from Lisbon and the south, with the probable

---

* " Vemos no reyno metter
  Tantos captivos crescer
  Irense os naturaes
  Que se assim tõr serão mais
  Elles que nós, a meu ver."

tinge of negro blood they had in them, must also
certainly have had a disposition, or predisposition, to
the animism so characteristic of the negro race.
Those who have known the negro on the coast of
Africa have all remarked the enormous place religion
—for it is just as hard to set the bounds between religion
and superstition as those of instinct and of reason, and
to say where the one finishes and the next begins—
holds in his mind and life.

His world is full of spirits—of the streams, the trees,
the dead. The living can dissociate their bodies from
their souls to plague the negro. He lives surrounded
by a world he cannot see, but feels in every action of
his life. Hence his belief in gri-gris, fetishes,* the
multiplicity of Ju-Ju houses, his human sacrifices,
witch doctors, and in some instances his cannibalism.
No race of men has ever been a fairer field for
missionary work. Theirs is a mind prepared to
listen to anyone who has a theory of the universe; to
listen and accept, and place the gods—for naturally
the negro looked upon the Trinity as three new beings
sent to him to adore—in his Pantheon.

No race of men ever, when once converted, sang
their hymns with greater fervour. The Methodist,
Wesleyan, Presbyterian, and generally all sects that
place faith over works, appealed to his imagination,
and marked him as their own. Curiously enough, the
Roman Catholics, though so successful with the
Indians of America, some of the races of the East, and
the Chinese, seem to have made but small appeal to
any of the races on the coast of Africa. The Mass,

* From the Portuguese " feitiço."

so awe-inspiring to the Indians, says little to the negro (of the Coast); but, on the contrary, seems to dissever him from all participation in the worship he attends. He likes to sing, to pray, and to perspire with fervour, and feel himself, as it were, in direct communication with his God. Faith, with the negro, is the sheet anchor, and what is the use, if the sheet anchor holds, of putting out a smaller holdfast anywhere ? Hence his neglect of works. That such is pretty nearly absolute, all those who know Jamaica, the Southern States of North America, or any other place where negroes have adopted any of the more animistic of the creeds of Protestantism, can testify.

Faith, to the negro nature, is a necessity of life. Good works do not appear to enter into his mental composition, and hence perhaps the curious likeness that is to be observed between so many of the religious movements that have arisen in Brazil and those of Asia Minor in the first and second centuries.

The Indian of Brazil has, with slight differences, the characteristics to be observed in all the Indians of America, outside the redskin tribes. We can but judge what kind of men the Tupis were by the crossbreeds that they have left, and by the Indians who to-day exist in various quarters of Brazil under conditions similar to theirs at the first conquest of the land. Still, it is to be observed, in judging men of savage races, who for three hundred years or more, as in Brazil, have lived under the knowledge and the menace of the whites, and usually have come in contact only with the scum of the white population on the frontiers, or with the soldiers sent against them in military expeditions, that they are certainly inferior to what they were three hundred years ago. Generally their chiefs and men of superior caste have been killed off, their daughters in the days of the first conquest often marrying whites, as in the case of Paraguassu, and the Inca princess who married Garcilaso de la Vega, and many other instances.

Often the wilder tribes exist in almost the same state as that in which the first historians of the Indies wrote of them, but having dropped the industries, which they were slowly struggling to a knowledge of, and gone back absolutely to a savage state.   This is especially to be noted in the case of a tribe known as the Pimentereios, who in the year 1760 suddenly made their appearance in the State of Piauhy.*   No one knew where they came from; for fifty years no Indians had been known in a wild state throughout the territory.   The Pimentereios soon made their presence felt by slaughtering cattle, burning isolated houses, and killing everyone they came across.   They kept the territory in alarm for years, till a Paulista,† one Domingos Jorge, exterminated many of them and forced the others to retire.   It was conjectured that these Indians were the descendants of a domesticated

* This State borders upon Pernambuco on the south and Maranhão on the north.

† The Paulistas were the inhabitants of São Paulo, a southern State.   Most of them at the time of Domingos Jorge had Indian blood.   Yet, under the name of Mamalucos, the Indians of the Jesuit Reductions in Paraguay never had enemies so bitter or so cruel.   The forays of the Paulistas in search of slaves forced the Jesuits to make their celebrated retreat with all their neophytes, a retreat which Father Ruiz Montoya has described so graphically that it has become almost the epic of the Guaranis.

tribe living near a place called Quebrobo, and that they had left a life of semi-civilisation to go back to the woods, having refused to fight against their wilder brethren, when called upon to do so by the whites. Should, therefore, any of them have survived to-day in a wild state, deep in the equatorial forests, it is clear that they must now be savager and less civilised than they were in the year 1760, after their short experience of settled life. The Indians of Brazil, left probably without their chiefs, and converted more or less by force, found in the Jesuits their best protectors against the colonists, who looked on them as merely beasts of burden, though, luckily for the Indians, at that time there were no mines discovered in Brazil, as there had been in nearly all the Spanish colonies. The Jesuits probably treated them somewhat as neophytes to be instructed in the faith—somewhat in the fashion of indentured labourers. At any rate, their yoke was preferable to that of the Paulistas or of the sugar-planters. The Jesuit system was to assemble as many Indians as they could in villages. In Paraguay, at least, where they had to deal with the gentle Guaranis, their rule was light, and now and then they winked at the Indians retaining pagan ceremonies, so that they had not anything cruel in them. In Brazil the Tupis were a harder race, and the settlements the Jesuits made never attained the great proportions of their Reductions in Paraguay,* although from the first conquests they laboured in the same way as they did in the former country.

* " E os ajuntaram em grandes alldeias."—" Annaes da Biblioteca Nacional," Rio de Janeiro, 1906.

Vicente Monteiro in his report to Mem de Sá, the Governor, talks of the Jesuits having been advised to gather up (the Indians) in large villages. As time went on and interbreeding both with the whites and negroes took place, the Indians in the villages gradually became absorbed into the civil population.

Their natural character, hard and suspicious, fierce and bloodthirsty, had not the time, that it had in Paraguay, to become modified under the Jesuit rule. No race in all the world is so impenetrable as is the Indian, in the reserve with which it arms itself against the ills of fortune, fights against tyranny or resists oppression, so to speak by enduring it without complaint. Such a race of men, reserved, suspicious, hospitable, vindictive, brave, cruel and hardy, taciturn in speech, and patient almost beyond the bounds of human patience, was almost certain to become imbued with strong religious faith. They had not, as had the negroes, a well-inhabited Pantheon, to which to add another deity or two was but a simple thing, for room was ample and the newcomer had full elbow-room. Their atmosphere, their trees, their rivers and their world in general contained no wealth of spirits. They had no Ju-Ju houses, and their fetishes were few, feeble, and far between. Their cast of mind was the least animistic, with the exception, possibly, of that of the Arabs, of any of the races of mankind. Their forms of worship were extremely simple, their dogmas simpler, consisting often of little more than some vague belief in a great spirit or of sun-worship. They used no human sacrifice in their religion*—at

* Cannibalism, though, was widely diffused amongst them.

least, the Indians of Brazil are not known ever to have
done so—and generally their ritual consisted in pouring out a calabash of water to the sun at daybreak, if
it was him that they adored.   None of them had
idols, nor do the Jesuits or the Franciscans, or any of
the missionaries who knew them at the conquest or
shortly afterwards, ever make mention of anything
approaching to what they certainly would have called
graven images.   Most of them seem to have believed
in a spirit of evil, to be propitiated in the usual way,
by offerings of fruit and flowers, of game, and
generally of anything the offerer had no great use for,
though in some cases he would offer up a favourite
bow, or blowpipe, and in extremity a finger from his
hand.   This spirit, who really had so much more
influence on their lives than his antagonist, the good
spirit, just as it often happens with ourselves, was
called Anhanga.   Their deity they named Tupán,
and as the early Jesuit missionaries say, gave almost
equal cult to the twin deities, although Tupán they
held as the creator of the world.   They nearly all
believed in the immortality of the soul; but that
belief seems to have had but little influence on their
lives, much in the same way that beliefs in general,
however strongly held, appear to spend themselves in
the mere action of belief, and are but seldom followed
by good deeds.   The Tupis seem to have come to a
comprehension of the true faith—that is to say, the
true faith as the Jesuits conceived it—not without
difficulty.

Baptism for a long time stuck in their throats,
although to us it seems a simple enough rite.   They

thought it likely to bring on coughs and colds, a not unreasonable* superstition, if the immersion plan was general amongst the missionaries. Smallpox was also almost certain to ensue after this fateful ceremony.

Father Lorenzana, writing of the Chaco tribes,† mentions a similar belief, and says that the poor Indian attacked by any illness imported from Europe sought to free himself from the effects of baptism by washing his head with sand, and scraping his tongue with a shell.

Occasionally, the Tupis after conversion altered the Catholic faith to what to them seemed natural, and Southey tells that a Jesuit complained that having delayed his visitation for two years, he found a chief had set up a new faith, in which the Blessed Virgin had become God's wife. The Jesuit complains that these "heretics" used the symbol of the cross, but without veneration, though he does not explain the way in which they lacked the veneration necessary.

All was put right as Southey tells us tartly, by the chief's death, "for his mythology perished with him." In fact, when the mad dog is dead the rabies also dies, as goes the adage, in Castilian.

Thus the conversion of the Tupis had its difficulties, and even then in their Malocas‡ were to be found the

* Southey, in his "History of Brazil," quotes this singular superstition from the works of a Jesuit.
† Lorenzana, "Gran Chaco de Gualamba."
‡ Maloca was the word used for the primitive Indian settlements. The houses were generally built in a square, round a central plaza, and communicated with one another. This form was adopted by the Jesuits in Paraguay, or allowed to remain, in their Reductions, and is to be seen still both in that country and Brazil.

germs of heresy, destined to bear its fruit in the religious history of Brazil.

What chiefly differentiated all the wild Indians of America from every other of the races of mankind was their attachment to their individual liberty.* Their chiefs seldom had great authority, and usually were chosen but for the duration of a war, and even then had no concern with anything but military things. Few of them were polygamists, and in the relationship between the sexes† were singularly strict, until the whites, in introducing the true faith amongst them, failed first to comprehend that faith themselves and then by their example broke down the tribal habits that had survived from the remotest ages of mankind, and gave the Indians no fixed rule of conduct that they themselves observed. This was a fact the better of the conquerors often realised, though usually upon their death-beds, as was the case with the last living of the conquerors of Peru who had accompanied Pizarro from the first setting out from Panama. This man, by name Marcio Serra de Lejesama, in his confession just before his death, addressed, as he says, to our Lord King Philip II. (1589), after rehearsing, as it were, the profession of his faith, and setting forth that all he did had been ill

* "Caboclo he so paro hoje" is a saying in the Sertão, meaning that one cannot count upon an Indian for more than one day, and that he will not be bound by his own employer to keep on working.

In his well-known "Down the Orinoco in a Canoe," Perez Triana tells of an Indian before whom he spread red baize and hatchets, gunpowder and knives—the wealth of Potosi to an Indian— to tempt him to engage to paddle for three days. All was in vain, and the Indian went off happy in his liberty.

† Padre Gumilla, in his "Orinoco Ilustrado," insists on this point.

done, puts on record, " that when we dispossessed these people of their lands, there was no thief in the whole territory, nor any maid or woman who was living an ill life." This done, he finished, saying, " I pray to God that He will pardon me, for I am the last to die of all the conquerors and the discoverers . . . and I now do what I can to relieve my conscience."*

There have been worse death-beds of more pious men than Lejesama was, and it is to be hoped his Lord did pardon him—that is, if even He had power to wipe out yesterday, making it even as to-day. Some few there were who did not need to pray upon their death-beds, except as we have all the need of it. Such were the good Lorenzano de Aldana, who came with Alvarado to Peru. He, in his will, left all his property to his Indians, in payment of their tribute in the future during their natural lives. He, with Alvar Nuñez Cabeça de Vaca, and Vasco Nuñez de Balboa, with a few more, were the bright spirits who rose superior to their times, by their humanity.

The witch-doctor, although an institution in almost all the Indian tribes, played a part far inferior to that played by the Gri-gri man amongst the negroes on the coast of Africa. The attitude of the converted Indian towards religion was widely different from that the negro always has assumed. Silent and introspective as he was, the Indian naturally took his

* This Lejesama was the man who, as his share of the Inca's treasure, was adjudged the golden sun from the Temple of the Sun in Cuzeo. He staked and lost it at a game of cards. Afterwards he never touched a card during his eventful life.

Repentance usually seems to have come to him tardily, as it does to most of us.

religion very seriously. No one has ever heard a
band of Indians singing hymns, and nothing of the
curious fervour of the negro ever attaches to him.
Upon the other hand, the " credo quia impossibilis "
is quite in his vein, and his priests usually find him
an obedient member of his Church.

The junction of such strangely different idiosyn-
crasies, dominated by the more potent strain brought
by the Portuguese, produced a religious caste of mind
specially suited to the growth of a rude Gnosticism.
Three centuries of isolation have given ample time
for its development. The Sertanejos have been all
that time cut off from the exterior world, partly
by circumstances and partly of their own free will.
Brazil, unlike most other countries of America, was
not first settled up on the sea coast or in the flat country
between it and the hills. The ports were built,
and sugar-planting entered into in the States, such
as Bahia, that lie within the tropics. Then the
peculiar configuration of the country, the spur of
enterprise—and the Portuguese of those days were
born explorers and discoverers—drew in the first place
expeditions to search for gold and silver across the
mountain ranges that run nearly along the whole
coast of Brazil at an average distance of about twenty
to nearly sixty miles ; then cattle-breeders followed
them. None of the mountains in Bahia exceed four
thousand feet in height. The passes never are more
than eighteen hundred to two thousand feet above the
level of the sea. Once past them, the region called
the Sertão begins, different in all respects from the
coastal plains.

The barrier of granitic gneiss, cut here and there by bands of sand and chalk, and dykes of eruptive basic rock, shut off the unknown interior from the first settlers.

The Indians of the coast received what gold they had from the tribes beyond the mountains. Occasionally an Indian from the interior coming to purchase salt, or drawn perhaps by the accounts he heard of the new race of bearded beings who rode strange animals that belched out fire and smoke,* would come and talk of the cool climate and the open plains beyond the hills. The people on the coast, sweltering in the tropic heat, shut in by the dense wall of vegetation that even still seems to throw a ring fence round the belt that stretches from the ocean to the hills, were naturally anxious to see the unknown country for themselves.

These adventures always proceeded on one plan. The adventurers formed themselves into a company, known in Brazilian Portuguese as a Bandeira. Those who formed the Bandeira contributed arms, money, food, and horses, according to their means ; from the Bandeira came the term " Bandeirante," so well known in the history of the conquest of Brazil. The leaders bore the name of Certanistas, and some of them had marvellous adventures, and have become half legendary, their exploits, curious and wild enough, having been mellowed and expanded under the micro-

---

* In many parts of America the Indians thought the horse and his rider were one flesh, and that the musket shots were flames breathed by the horse, so that to them, literally, his neck was clothed with thunder.

scope of time.   Nothing is commoner than to hear a
Fazendeiro,* either in São Paulo or Bahia, say : " My
ancestor was a Bandeirante."   It gives him, as it were, a
halo, just as with us to be descended from a Norman
baron or a Highland Chief imparts a status often as
difficult of proof.

Still, many of the expeditions of the Bandeirantes
are historical, and the adventures they encountered
and the privations they endured are truly marvellous,
especially of those who penetrated the mountain
barrier in the first settlement of São Paulo, and of the
distant Matto Grosso, whose fastnesses are little
known, even at the present day.

Most of these Bandeirantes were Paulistas—that is,
inhabitants of São Paulo—an adventurous race, who
from the first have set their seal upon Brazil.

As far back as the middle of the sixteenth century
a Bandeirante, one Aleixo Garcia, with his brother
and a small expedition, crossed the continent, and
passing through what is now Paraguay, reached to
the foothills of the Andes, a journey that seems
hardly possible, given the difficulties he had to meet
with, the absolutely unknown country that he had to
cross, the enormous distance, and the tribes of savage
Indians through whose territories he was obliged to
pass   One almost fancies that, like Fray Marcos de
Niza, the bold friar who set out from Southern
California and reached the Pueblos on the Rio
Grande, visiting Zuñi and describing it with the strange
customs of the Indians, he must " have followed where

* Fazendeiro is a man who has a fazenda—that is, an estate ; thus
fazendeiro equals landowner.

the Holy Ghost did lead." Few expeditions in the history of the opening up of a new territory have undergone more hardships than the brief records of the Bandeiras have preserved for us. The first Bandeiras that left the coast had but the vaguest notions of the route they had to take to pass across the hills. A year or two, or even three years, was an ordinary time for them to be away wandering amongst the woods, crossing great rivers, scaling hills, harassed by constant Indian attacks, a prey to every kind of insect that makes life a burden in the wilderness of never-ending trees, all bound together with lianas, thorny and hostile to mankind. Gold was the lodestar that drew them into the interior, but for full one hundred years they never found it, till at last, one Bartolomeo Bueno struck the rich mining regions of Goyaz, after three years of ineffectual effort, and of miseries. Two of the best known Bandeirantes were Englishmen, and figure as Antonio Kinvet and Henrique Barroway in the annals of the time.*

Antonio and Henrique seem to have been what they no doubt styled "free-traders," and the Brazilian probably more bluntly called pirates, for they were taken prisoners in a "Corsario Inglez," and long detained in prison, either on account of their heretical opinions or their piratical exploits, or an admixture of the two. Being released, they joined the Bandeira of Correa de Sá in 1597, and had incredible adventures in the interior. They settled down at last, as mere cattle farmers, and probably married Tupi women,

---

* "Revista do Instituto Historico do Rio de Janeiro," vol. ii., 1878.

especially as Pedro Vas de Caminha, in his celebrated letter to the King in 1580, refers to these ladies as " Moças bem gentis," and says in grace they owed but little to the Lisbon girls.

By slow degrees the Sertão was peopled, and as the climate was much cooler than the coast, the settlers gradually began to raise large herds of cattle and of goats. The country, although not open as in the provinces of Parana and Rio Grande, was rich in little plains hemmed in by belts of scrub. These were the lands now known as the Caatingas, famous for cattle-breeding. Thus the interior was sooner settled up than was the coast, which to this day, as is to be observed even outside the capital, is shut off from the mountains by a dense belt of the primeval forest, giving to those who go no further a false view of the country, in which civilisation seems to end in the vast waves of jungle that stretch on every side. The real Brazilians of the old school, the true descendants of the intrepid Bandeirantes, are only to be found in the interior. There they still live a semi-patriarchal life, and are but little touched by all the changes which render those who live in towns subject to constant changes that cut them off in sentiment from the generations that preceded them. In the long-drawn-out expeditions of the Bandeirantes, the character of the Brazilian race must have been slowly forming, as they passed their lives struggling to penetrate the unknown interior.

As European women seldom or never accompanied the first discoverers, they formed alliances with the Indians, and as they pushed back further from the

coast, much fewer opportunities arose to mix their
blood with the black race, and thus their children
nearly all became what were termed Mamalucos—that
is, half white, half Indian—inheriting on the one side
the Portuguese tendency to mysticism, and on the
other the melancholy and introspection of the Indian,
rendering them susceptible to that fanaticism which
has so often manifested itself in Pernambuco and
Bahia during the last three hundred years.

Indians and negroes alike seem to have fallen
victims to it, manifesting their differing racial
characteristics in the various outbreaks of religious
mania that have taken place. These outbursts were,
after all, not so much to be wondered at when the
religious history of Portugal itself is studied carefully. Nothing of the same kind ever took place in
Spain; the materialistic character of its inhabitants preserved them from outbreaks of that sort. Hermits and
saints Spain has produced in quantities, but Spanish
history does not seem to contain any account of
movements such as that headed by the mystical
fanatic known as the King of Penamacor, or that
headed by the man who styled himself the King of
Ericeira. Both of these worthies, followed by a crowd
of their disciples, betook themselves to solitary places
in the hills, wandering about, subsisting more or less
on locusts and wild honey, passing the day in listening
to their leaders preach, the night often in singing hymns
and in debauchery. Their faith was quite undoubted.
Their actions did not seem to them to matter so
long as they maintained their faith. Thus did the
followers of Montanus and Carpocrates act, in the

second century. "Mysticism," Renan says in his
"L'Eglise Chrétienne," "has always been a moral
danger, for it allows [people] to think too easily that
by initiation a man is freed from ordinary duties."*

The Gnostics were reported to have held, perhaps
by their enemies, that things of the flesh are fleshly,
things of the soul are spiritual. This axiom once
accepted, any kind of conduct is right; or, perhaps,
to put it accurately, all kinds of conduct, for a man
who conforms to it may be an ascetic one day and
a libertine the next, until advancing age makes him
indifferent to both.

Akin to these outbreaks of religious illumination
under the two "Kings," was the politico-mystic creed
of the Sebastianists.† This sect, extinct in Portugal,
in Brazil survived down to the year 1896, and
possibly survives up to the present day. Thus did the
Portuguese come well prepared for spiritual adventures
to the New World. Mysterious flames that issued
from caverns in the hills, coffins that floated in the air
over the palaces of kings, shadowy battalions of Moors
clothed in burnouses, who at due intervals appeared

---

* "Le mysticisme a toujours été un danger moral, car il laisse
trop facilement entendre que par l'initiation en est dispensé des
devoirs ordinaires."—"L'Eglise Chrétienne," p. 162.

† In my youth I remember an old man who was believed to be a
Sebastianist, but he may have had as much madness as Sebastianism
in his composition. He used to wander up and down the Province
of the Minho, and into Galicia, and sit upon a rock, gazing out sea-
ward for the coming of the fleet of Don Sebastian. Such faith
certainly might have removed a chain of mountains, but did not, as
far as I know, bring the King into his own again. However, the
poor old Sebastianist, no doubt, had his reward, for faith is the best
anodyne to common sense—that common sense which makes the
world a desert to Sebastianists.

and often joined in aerial battles with Christian paladins, were but as commonplaces in their lives. The werwolf (Lobis-Homen), the evening sprite (O tardo), and the rest of the remains of Pagan polytheism, played a great part amongst the peasants of the Minho, and the Traz os Montes, as they do even to-day, imbuing them with mysticism, superstition, or primitive religion, according to the point of view from which they are approached.

Nor were the negroes much behind them. Their child-like, bloody creeds, indeed, took a far different complexion. For them, as with some Christian sects, the blood was everything, and they would well have understood the Scottish minister of a bygone age who said, " If ye tak' out the blood from it, I would na' tak' the trouble of carrying the Book home."

The Hausa negroes, in Bahia, added to the Christian creed the Jorubana ritual, and introduced their fetish worship into the services of the Church, just as in Haiti, Santo Domingo, and some say even in Jamaica, Obi and Voodoo worship still prevail amongst the negroes on the sly. Those who have seen their agapemones in which after a religious service they abandon themselves to all the licence of the phallic dance at their Candombles, can testify how well adapted are they for all kinds of religious mania, enthusiasm, revivalism, or anything that puts them into that state of excitation of the senses in which the mind ceases to work or works subservient to the nerves. In Pajehu, a district in the State of Pernambuco, there stands a mountain in the range known as the Serra Talhada, which dominates the country for

miles on every side. A grey, granitic mass, it has
something majestic in its appearance, towering up
from the plain. In it there is an isolated block,
shaped something like a pulpit, known as A Pedra
Bonita—that is, the Pretty Stone. This place in 1837
was the theatre of scenes which recall all the worst
atrocities of the Ashantis, in their devil worship.* In
1837 a Cafuz, some say a Mamaluco, but anyhow
a religious monomaniac, what is called an Illuminado
in Portuguese, and in Spanish an Alumbrado, collected most of the population of the neighbouring
villages. Who he was is still uncertain, but evidently
he was possessed of what is requisite on such occasions
—faith in himself and an interminable flow of words.
It is possible his faith was genuine, for who shall
judge the heart ? Of one thing there can be no doubt:
his sermons were interminable. Mounting upon the
block of stone, he stood, a new world, John of Leyden,
preaching the coming of the King Don Sebastian, he
who fell at the field of Alcazar-el-Kebir. He foretold that the stone should be cut into steps ; not cut
with any earthly tools, but smoothed away by the
shedding of the blood of children. Up these steps, so
miraculously to be prepared, surrounded by his guard
of honour, dressed in armour, the King, who had been
dead three hundred years, should ascend and come
into his own again, reigning in Portugal and in Brazil,
and bountifully rewarding those who had been faithful
to him, and by their faith contributed to his dis-
enchantment. No more was wanted; the whole

---

* Euclydes da Cunha describes it in his book, "Os Sertoẽs," Rio
de Janeiro, 1917.

Sertão, from Pajehu right to the Rio das Egoas, in Pernambuco, Piauhy, Bahia and Ceará, was all convulsed. A nervous agitation seemed to communicate itself to everybody. The rude Vaqueiros, all dressed in leather, with their stiff coats made of deer's hide, their long hard leggings, and their low round hats, giving them an air of medieval men-at-arms, arrived from every side. Mounted upon their fiery little horses, and riding at the medieval amble —which is so easy that the rider may carry in his hand a glass of water and spill no drop of it—bearing their flint-lock wide-mouthed Bacamortes across their saddles, girt with a rusty sword, or with the long, sharp-pointed knife they call a jacaré,* or faca de Parnyba stuck in their sashes, they came, and then sat sideways on their horses listening to the preacher, and believed. Belief with them was easy as it so often is if the thing to be believed is unbelievable. Negroes and half-castes of all shades of colour, Indians, Cafuces, Mamalucos, Caboclos, and men of every one of the bewildering shades of colour, flocked to the Pretty Stone. A multitude of women, all a prey to the mysterious agitation which in such cases, whether at revivals in Port Glasgow, camp meetings in the United States, or pilgrimages to holy places in Calabria, seems to transform them, making them just as irresponsible as the Bacchantes of the older world, came through the mountain passes, followed the trails through virgin forests and assembled to hear the word

---

* Jacaré is a Guarani word, and means alligator. Faca de Parnhyba = knife from Parnhyba. A blunderbuss in Portuguese is called a " Bracamorte."

preached at the wondrous pulpit made by no earthly hands. Unluckily they brought their children with them. Then, roused to a religious frenzy beyond belief, as they stood listening to the words of the illuminated Cafuz or Mamaluco—for history has not preserved his name—women strove with one another who should be the first to offer up her child, so that its blood should split the rock and form the sacred stair, by which the King, the long lamented Don Sebastian, should ascend in glory, bringing back peace and plenty upon earth.

A common-sense but accurate historian* says that for days the rocks ran blood. This man, devoid of faith and quite incapable of rising to the comprehension of heights to which the Cafuz (or Mamaluco) had transported his rapt hearers, informs us when the " lugubrious farce "† was over that so great was the quantity of blood shed by the faithful the place became pestiferous and had to be deserted, until a purifying Nature worked a cure upon it. The events which happened at A Pedra Bonita were perhaps the most appalling of any in the history of Brazil; but long before that, in the seventeenth century, in the mountain chain of Piquaraçá near Jacobina, in Bahia, a missionary, one Apollonio de Todi, coming from a mission in the north, was so much struck with the resemblance of the mountain to Mount Calvary that he resolved to build a chapel there. Luckily for the children of those times the missionary was neither

---

* Araripe Junior, in his " Reino Encantado."
† " Lugubre farça " is the term used by Euclydes da Cunha, in his description of the sacrifice in his book " Os Sertoës."

a Cafuz or Mamaluco, but only a well-meaning, visionary friar. His first proceeding was to change the name Piquaraçá to Monte Santo. Then, preaching to the rude Sertanejos, he stirred them up, not to the pitch of human sacrifice, but to assist him in his scheme. So well he worked, and so well was he seconded by the impressionable folk of the Sertão, that in a short time on the summit of the highest peak an enormous church was built.

Up to it, cut out of the solid rock, this time with ordinary picks and shovels, a Via Sacra of three kilometres led, with five-and-twenty little oratories as stations of the cross. Nothing was wanted but a miracle to make the place respectable and to bring pilgrims to it from all the country round. The faithful Sertanejos had not long to wait, for in due course some mystic letters of gigantic size, an A, an L and S, topped by a cross, were found cut in the rock.

The Sertanejos did the rest, throwing their faith and simple piety into the common stock; thus Monte Santo soon became renowned.

In Holy Week, when from remote villages in the Sertão the Vaqueiros and their families crowd to the holy fair, the scene recalls the Middle Ages. Such orgasms of piety, such wild intensity of faith, are rarely to be seen in a world where the educated turn for their spiritual consolation rather to crystal-gazing or to palmistry than to such vulgar superstitions as satisfy the simple herdsmen of the Sertão.

The scene is marvellous, with its myriad camp fires, its herds of horses grazing loose or picketed, the strange, old-fashioned, medieval types of men, and the vast panorama extending over leagues of mountains, oceans of tropic forest, and with the glittering sea in the far distance, its surf-lashed beach encircled round by palms. Preacher succeeds to preacher, and under the wild eloquence of some illuminated friar, or inspired herdsman, by degrees excitement stirs the multitude into an excess of pious fervour, that recalls scenes that took place when first the faith was spread amongst the Gentiles, or when Mohammed stirred the souls of the rude Arabs in the wilds of the Hejaz.

The friar Apollonio had no successor of like genius with himself, although at intervals some Mamaluco or Cafuz arises and strives to emulate him.

The last and greatest of them all was that Antonio Conselheiro whose life and miracles, as the phrase goes in Lives of saints, I hope this Introduction may explain, or at least make possible of comprehension to those who never heard of him, or of the curious region where he lived, preached, and succeeded for a brief interval, and then, having set up for a redeemer, as the Castilian bitter saying has it, met the redeemer's fate.

CHAPTER I

In 1889, when the Emperor Don Pedro II. gave up his throne and the republic was proclaimed, it was inevitable that in remote and medieval districts, such as the Sertão, there would be still left many, hostile to the new form of government.

Not only were the new ideas repugnant to them, but they were almost incomprehensible to men who, though the actual government was never very manifest to them in their daily lives, still held the patriarchal theory of life in its entirety.

It is not to be supposed they had any excessive loyalty towards Don Pedro as a man ; but they most probably conceived him as something indispensable. Just as their priests looked to the Pope as their spiritual head and chief, without, in the Sertão, troubling a great deal as to his existence, so did the Sertanejos look upon their Emperor. The priests, moreover, would be certain to inculcate in them a respect for monarchy, partly from personal, partly from ecclesiastical feelings of use and wont. The Church, we know, adapts itself to every form of government, seeing at once that if it can bend or enslave (according to the reader's point of view) the mind, all the rest is merely leather and prunella, and that the republican may contribute to the offertory as freely as the best believer in the Divine right of kings.

This feeling of uneasiness in regard to the new government, the mysticism of the people as shown in the belief in the return to earth of Don Sebastian, and the fear that the republic meant the destruction of all religion, tended to make the dwellers in the Sertão especially susceptible to any movement, religious or political alike, during the time between the abdication of the Emperor and the firm establishment of the new government. Out of the depths of superstition and of violence, Antonio Conselheiro arose to plunge the whole Sertão into an erethism of religious mania and of blood.

His ancestors were men of violence, although no doubt fervent believers ; subservient to their priests ; singers of " novenas " in their houses, honourers of their fathers and their mothers, and in fact not much unlike the Scottish Highlanders of the sixteenth century, except that they were far more fervent in their faith. To complete the likeness, the Emperor's writ had as little force in the Sertão as had the King's beyond the Pass of Aberfoyle in the days of Rob Roy.

Though in Bahia modern life was well established, with telegraphs and telephones and public lighting of the streets and tramways only two hundred miles away, these things were quite unknown and almost unsuspected by the ordinary man. The Sertanejo when he went to town—and town to him was not Bahia, but Joazeiro, Jacobina, Queimadas, or some other little local centre—passed his sword between his saddle girths, and either wore a pair of antique pistols at his saddle bow, or carried in his hand a flintlock blunderbuss. He never stirred from home except armed to the teeth, and even in his home, when he put on his hat, he also stuck his "jacaré"* into his belt.

So was the Highlander of old a being distinct from any Lowlander by the fact of always going armed. As Addison and Rob Roy McGregor flourished at the same time, so did Antonio Conselheiro and the scientific Emperor, Don Pedro de Alcantara, pursue their differing avocations at the same moment, in Brazil. As often happens in back-lying† districts, powerful families pursued their feuds, and levied war upon each other. Such was the custom up to the other day, in Western Texas, Kentucky, in Calabria, in the Province of Valencia in Spain, and in Corsica. Although the Sertão extends to several States of the Republic of Brazil, as Bahia, Pernambuco, Ceará and Piauhy, the customs are identical in all the States, and the Sertanejo rather looks upon himself as such, than as an inhabitant of the different provinces. Thus, in the Sertão of Ceará in the wild districts that lie between Quixeramobim and Tamboril, the families of the Maciel and Araujos kept all the country in confusion with their feuds. Antonio Conselheiro sprang from the family of Maciel.

The Maciels‡ were poor but numerous, and maintained themselves by cattle-raising upon a minor scale. They seem to have been also small landowners, and, as

* Long knife. Literally, "alligator"—from the Guarani word meaning an alligator.
† This Scottism avoids the odious German "hinterland."
‡ "Maciel," plural "Macieis" in Portuguese.

4

contemporaries aver, all of them active and athletic men, living the ordinary life of the Vaqueiros, dressing in leather and always going armed. The Araujos presumably were but little superior to them in education and in culture. Their daily life was similar to that of the Maciels—their dress, their habit of always carrying arms, and their religious faith. The difference was in their possessions, for the Araujos clan were landowners and cattle-breeders on a large scale.

Their houses probably were such as I have often seen throughout the country districts of Brazil. They stood most likely surrounded by a clump of mango or of orange trees, long, low and yellow, with red-tiled roofs such as one still can see in Brazil and in the remoter parts of Portugal, and dated possibly from the early days of the settlement of the Sertão. Behind them stretched a field or two of Indian corn or mandioca (known as a " roza "), with stumps of trees, cut off or burned, dotted throughout the crop. The Caatinga* probably came close up to the corrals for cows, on one side, and at the front a little plain, studded with stunted palms, stretched out ; and on it fed their cattle, their mules and horses, and probably some goats.

There may have been a little grove either of bananas or guayabas, and a tall palm or two about the house. From the corrals an acrid smell would be wafted on the air, not disagreeable when you are used to it, and not unlike the smell of peat that hangs about a Highland shieling in the remoter glens. The

* Bush, in Guarani.

house itself most certainly had something Oriental in its configuration and its air. Passing the fence and the various hitching-posts where you tied up your horse, you came to the front door, made like a door in Portugal or Spain, to revolve upon a solid hinge stuck into a socket in the lintel—a fashion which the Moors had left in the Peninsula. In default of iron, the lock most likely was of wood, just as locks used to be in Fez, ten or twelve years ago. The front door opened to the saguán, the passage to the inner court, found in all ancient houses, whether in Portugal or Spain, or in their colonies. Rooms lay to right and left of the courtyard, and in them there would be two or three ancient leather-seated, high-backed chairs, around a table of hard, dark-coloured wood. Upon it stood a porous water-vessel with a dew exuding from its sides, flanked by a heavy silver cup or two. Six or seven Lives of saints, printed at Coimbra, and bound in vellum, with ties and eyelets (to which shells worn smooth by handling acted as buttons), together with a Book of Hours, would form the library.

Two or three negro slaves and a dozen yellow dogs were certain to be lounging near the front door, or just outside the fence. To complete the Oriental air, you might have stayed a week within the house and never seen the women, although you heard them and felt certain that they had reconnoitred you a hundred times, through holes you could not see.

The Araujos, or any family who owned a house such as that I have just described, would live in homely style, but plentifully. Their flocks and herds, with their tilled fields and groves of oranges and of bananas, provided them with food. Food was abundant, if not luxurious, for every now and then they killed a bullock, drying the best part of the meat in long, thin strips, which was called " charqui " in the plains, and in the Sertão " carne do vento," which literally means " wind meat," or meat dried in the wind. This meat dried in the sun or wind is not unpalatable when fried or done up in a stew that the Brazilians call " angú," composed of charqui and of rice with bits of pumpkin on the top of it. The whole is piled up in a pyramid upon the dish, and looks a little like the stews used by the Moors throughout North Africa. The men assembled in the dining-room and sat about a long, rough table in patriarchal style, the elders at the top. Mulatto girls, with their chemises slipping off their shoulders and shoes like those worn by the Moors that slap upon the ground with the movement of the foot, bore in the dinner, carrying it high above their heads in platters made of earthenware or wood, or perhaps silver in the richer families. The stew discussed, black beans and bacon followed; this dish is called " feijão," and takes the place that porridge does in Scotland, the soup in France, or macaroni with Italians, in every household in Brazil. Fine mandioca flour is powdered over it to make it thicker and more palatable. This flour is often called " farinha do pão," that is, the flour of wood, and tastes like sawdust to palates not attuned to it, but is most nourishing. After the beans and bacon and the stew, rice boiled in milk and powdered thick with cinnamon was served, just as day follows night, and quite as certainly. Sometimes this would be varied by " cangica," that is, maize boiled in milk, held a great delicacy, and so much appreciated in Brazil that country people have a saying, "Cangica knocks out every kind of dish."* When all was over, home-made cigars or cigarettes, rolled in the husks of corn, were lighted, and a girl came in carrying a silver basin full of water and a long towel with fringed ends to dry the hands upon, after they were washed in Oriental style by pouring water upon them. Strong native coffee and " cachaza," that is, white rum made from the sugar-cane, most probably at home, would finish the repast. Then the guests would retire each to his hamac for the siesta, which occupied an hour or two. After the evening meal, they all assembled to sing the Rosary, and then retired to rest. If in the morning after you got up (always at daylight) you met a negro either in the passages or just outside the door, he seized your hand and kissed it, or asked your blessing, which you bestowed as solemnly as possible; for to have refused would have been a dire offence, both to the man himself and to good manners; and on good manners the older generation of Brazilians, so to speak, built their Church.

Few flowers were grown, except in the richest houses, and even then they generally were the Marvel of Peru, or some luxuriant creeper that climbed upon the walls. Pumpkins were the chief vegetables upon the cattle farms, though near the coast they were more plentiful, as sweet potatoes, okross, and many others, familiar to Brazil.

* " A cangica borra Todo."

These patriarchal folk, though they lived simply, were full of pride of race and family, and kept a hold upon the local magistracy with a grip of iron. Thus when the Araujos found their ascendancy was not acknowledged by the Maciels, their fury knew no bounds.

Colonel João Brigido dos Santos has left us an account of how the feud began, and it is interesting as it serves to show from what stock Antonio Conselheiro sprang. In the fashion of most of these clan feuds, whether in the Scottish Highlands of old or elsewhere, the carrying off of cattle furnished the first excuse.

Colonel dos Santos describes the heads of the family of Maciel as " vigorous and sympathetic men, of good appearance, truthful and serviceable," and hints that the accusations brought against them by the Araujos were not based on proofs, but merely formed a pretext, and that the real reason of their enmity was that the Maciels, though poor, contested the supremacy of the richer family. That may have been ; but what is certain is that the Araujos for real or fancied wrongs got all their clan together and fell upon their foes. Contrary to general expectation, they were repulsed with loss.

The Maciels had gathered all their partisans and were prepared to carry fire and sword into the terri-tories of the enemy. As all this happened in 1833, it gives a picture of the life in the Sertão at that time, and is identical with that upon the Scottish border in the days of James I. Substitute Johnstone and Jardine for Araujo and Maciel, and take the scene from the drought-cursed Sertão to the damp wilds of Durisdeer or Annandale, and the resemblance is complete.

The Araujos, after their defeat, a prey to rage and disappointment, and either fearing or being unwilling to engage in further open strife, looked about for men to whom to delegate their vengeance and their hate. Such men are never hard to find, even to-day, in the Sertão.

José Joaquin de Menezes, a man from Pernambuco, renowned for deeds of violence and blood, and a well-known bravo, one Vicente Lopes of Aracaguassú, offered their services. These rascals, under the leadership of a certain Sylvestre Rodrigues Veras, a relation of Araujo da Costa, chief of the clan, collected all their friends and followers and fell upon their enemies by night. They stealthily surrounded the house where lived the chief of the Maciels. As all resistance was impossible, the Araujos sent in a man to say that they would spare the lives of the Maciels if they surrendered without fight. They, taken by surprise, agreed, after they had secured a promise of their lives. As was to be expected, the promise was not kept. At the end of the first day's journey, the prisoners were murdered in cold blood. Amongst them was Antonio Maciel, the headman of his clan. This man was a grandfather of Antonio Conselheiro, and appears to have been quite innocent of the cattle robberies of which he was accused. So, at least, says Manoel Ximenes in his " Memorias," almost the only documentary evidence of these curious events that has been preserved to us.

Antonio's uncle, Miguel Carlos, managed to escape.

Bound as he was and with his legs secured under his horse's belly, his flight seems difficult to account for, unless, as happened to Rob Roy McGregor in a like plight, he had a friend amongst his adversaries to untie his bonds for him.

Whether this was the case or not, one thing is certain, that the pursuit of him was instant and well sustained. The pursuers all were mounted on their best horses, and all were men accustomed to every phase of frontier life. As I have heard a tracker in the upper provinces of the Argentine Republic say of himself, to them " the desert was an open book." Most likely all of them could follow up a trail at a short "lope," without dismounting, when it ran clear on open ground. To such men, all spurred on by hope of vengeance and by hate, the capture of the fugitive was a certainty. He, having been joined by his sister, as good a frontierman as he himself, and a skilled markswoman, employed all the ruses of a hunted man upon the frontier. The brother and sister waded down streams, turned back upon the trail, confused it by treading in each other's footsteps, and by dragging boughs in their hands behind them. They fired the grass in front of them and crossed the burnt up patches, stepping on stones and branches of burnt trees. All was in vain ; at last, exhausted, they hid themselves in a deserted hut.

In a short time their enemies appeared like hounds on a hot scent. Day was just breaking, when the intrepid brother and sister stood at bay, determining to sell their lives at the best price.

Miguel Carlos was wounded in the foot. In spite

of that, with his gun in his hand and a sharp-pointed knife between his teeth, he stood before his sister in the door to face his enemies. His first shot killed one Theotonio, whose body fell against the open door, preventing it from being closed. As she was struggling to close it, and drag away the body of the dead man, the sister fell, pierced by a bullet in the breast. Then Pedro Veras, the leader of the attacking party, rushed forward, only to fall pierced by a load of slugs fired from a blunderbuss from the inside of the hut. This gave Miguel Carlos a moment's respite, which he took full advantage of, maintaining a hot fire. The next act was that to be expected in a frontier fight —the attackers managed to set the roof on fire.

The man inside, now rendered desperate, also recurred to an old frontier ruse. Filling an earthen jar with water, he dashed it on the flames. Immediately a dense steam arose. Covered by it, and firing as he ran, his knife in his left hand, he sprang across the body of his sister, and bounding through the circle of his foes, disappeared into the woods. Either the besiegers had had enough of slaughter, or Miguel Carlos Maciel had covered up his tracks so well that they did not pursue him, but if they did they failed to find his trail. It may be that they held him not worthy of pursuit, as a mere "Pe Rapado," literally a shaven foot, or vagabond, not able to do harm.

In this they were deceived, for some months afterwards, one of the Araujo family on his way to church to marry a rich lady of those parts fell mortally wounded by a bullet, fired from an ambush by Miguel Carlos, who thus avenged his sister and his friends.

Another sister, Helena Maciel, then joined him and was invaluable to him by giving due notice of his enemies' designs.

Brother and sister lived hidden in the woods, although at times they came out boldly and killed or tried to kill such of their enemies as exposed themselves. On one occasion, in a little country store, Miguel Carlos met a man who he suspected was a spy set on him by his enemies. He instantly made friends with him, and as they rode out of the town, at the first corner, Miguel Carlos buried a knife between his shoulders and left him dead upon the road.

Innumerable were the adventures and crimes in which Miguel Carlos and his sister were involved, but as the swimmer in the end is always taken by the sea —at least, so says the Arab proverb—his fate was certain, in such a place as the Sertão.

One day he went to bathe in a stream near a little town called Cotovello, accompanied by several of his friends. After their bathe they sat down on the sand to dress themselves, when suddenly out of a thicket of tall reeds appeared a band of the Araujos, who opened fire upon them. His friends, seizing their clothes, plunged into the thickest of the reeds, leaving Miguel Carlos alone upon the beach.

Dressed only in his drawers and with a knife held in his hand, he ran towards a house amidst a shower of bullets, which all missed their mark. He reached the house, opened the door, and fell mortally wounded, but still holding fast his knife. One Manoel de Araujo, chief of the band of murderers, stabbed him as he lay. With his last breath Miguel Carlos bounded to his feet, and buried his knife deep in his adversary's throat.

The two fell dead, one on the other, and Helena Maciel, rushing up fully armed, stamped on the face of her brother's murderer and managed to escape. For long she ranged the country like a fury, and once more murdered another victim to avenge her brother's death. This was the last of her exploits, and this time she did not execute her vengeance personally, but left it to a band of paid assassins, who fell upon a relation of the Araujos and beat him so barbarously that he died. Helena appears to have been satisfied that she had done enough, and lived quite unmolested to a good old age.

The quarrel still went on, and the two families for many years slaughtered each other quite impartially. One of the few survivors was Vicente Mendes Maciel, father of Antonio Conselheiro, who does not appear to have been engaged in following up the feud.

Colonel João Brigido* describes him as an irascible man, but of great probity, half a visionary and suspicious in the extreme. He must have been a man of some capacity, though quite illiterate, in spite of which he entered largely into business, keeping all his accounts and records of his affairs by memory, as he could neither read nor write nor had the slightest knowledge of arithmetic. In such surroundings did the young Antonio Mendes Maciel grow up, seeing on every side of him deeds of violence and blood. The country where he lived was certainly a curious school

* "Crimes celebres do Ceará. Os Araujos e Macieis."

for a young man, such as he was, to have been born
into.   His uncles all had been concerned in the
fierce feud with the Araujos, and thus no doubt
he imbibed a hatred of the rich.   Some of his
nearest relatives had fallen in the feud, and so his
earliest recollections must have been tinged with
thoughts of vengeance.   At the same time, most of
the combatants, upon both sides, were probably men
imbued with deep religious feelings, of a peculiar
kind.   They all believed in omens, and in a way were
mystics, or at the least were visionaries, seeing supernatural intervention in natural events, and with the
names of Jesus and the saints always upon their lips.

All this prepared him, without doubt, for a life
singularly unlike that of a man born in the nineteenth
century.   His education was superior to that of his
relations, received most likely from the priests, who
certainly would inculcate hatred of republican ideas,
fealty to monarchy, and a regard to old traditions of
whatever kind they were.   His reading certainly was
confined to Lives of saints, books on religion, and the
breviary.

Sebastianism he found in the air of the Sertão.
Nobody questioned it, and the whole life he led drew
him to mysticism.   All seems to have worked together to prepare a man certain to be remarkable in
the Sertão, when once he had emerged from his
obscurity.

CHAPTER II

Antonio Vicente Mendes Maciel was born in the Sertão of Ceará in a little town called Quixeramobim, somewhere about the year 1842; but the date is not known with certainty. The sobriquet of Conselheiro (the Councillor) he acquired in later years, after he had risen to fame in the Sertão.

He seems to have been well educated, that is to say in relation to the circumstances in which he was brought up. Like many men destined in after life to prominence amongst their fellows, he was a timid and retiring youth, averse from mixing with his playmates and with other boys. His father employed him as a cashier or manager in his store at Quixeramobim, and he appears rarely to have left the paternal home, where he discharged his duties with fidelity and care.

The irascibility of his father never seems to have manifested itself in the son's character, in his quiet youth, or in the stirring scenes which he was destined to take part in during his chequered life. On the contrary, his temper seems to have been quite imperturbable, steadfast and quiet, with a good share of the inevitable obstinacy with which all martyrs must be plentifully endowed.

Although he surely must have heard his father

talking with his friends about the tragic history of the family a thousand times, Antonio Maciel does not appear to have been affected in the least by it, as far as it is known. He bore the character of a retiring youth, occupied solely with his father's business affairs. His days passed at the desk, and nothing seems to have preoccupied him, except the care of his three sisters, left, by his father's death in 1855, entirely in his charge.

Imagination pictures him, dressed in drill trousers and an alpaca coat, seated absorbed with the small details of a village store, his recreations a walk round the plaza in the evening, or a rare visit, on a pacing mule, to a country neighbour a league or two away.

His real life most certainly was of the spirit ; and in the little church, built of adobe, with its little bell-cote over the east door, no doubt he knelt for hours in ecstasy before the " Bom Jesus," His " Blessed Mother," or " San Antonio," that sainted son of Portugal. He would be sure to turn up at any neighbour's house during " novenas " and sing the hymns with fervency, and in his home never forget the rosary before he went to bed.

Life in a small Brazilian town leaves ample time for contemplation, and no doubt when any preaching friar came round upon a mission, the quiet and retir- ing storekeeper was at his ministrations, hanging on his words. The town itself afforded but few recrea- tions, and they were not the kind of recreation that would have attracted him. A cock-fight on a Sunday, and now and then what was called an " encamisada," when the young men, mounted on their best horses, fought a mock combat, with one side dressed in white to represent the Moors, a medieval custom brought from Portugal, were the amusements of the place, descended from old times. Sometimes they must have ridden at the ring on holidays; but this was not a sport in which the introspective, self-absorbed young man would have been likely to engage.

Nothing, up to the year 1858, gave any sign that the careful storekeeper would be called upon to play the part that fate had destined for him on his remote and lonely stage. No doubt the blood of his wild family but slumbered, and though it never manifested itself in the same fashion as it did with his uncles and his grandfather, the taint was certain to appear.

His marriage in the year 1858 transformed him utterly. The habits of a quiet life were thrown aside, and he embarked on a career of wandering and change of scene that in the end made him an outcast, and perhaps unhinged his mind. His wife, whose name history has not preserved, seems to have been utterly unsuited to him. Of violent temper and loose character, it seems impossible that such a sober-minded youth could have fallen in love with her, except, perhaps, in the same way that an old maid is sometimes taken with a rake. Her very difference from himself may have attracted him.

From the first, his wife seems to have indulged in love affairs. Time after time he pardoned her. It was no use, for, as the Spanish proverb has it, the she goat will be off into the woods.*

* "La Cabra tira al monte."

Whether to take his wife away from evil company, or because of the notoriety attaching to her excursions into the realms of Cytherea, Antonio Maciel left the paternal store and town in 1859, and went to a town called Sobral, where once again he found employment as a cashier.   There for a time he duly entered sacks of black beans and mandioca flour, tobacco and jerked beef, hogsheads of sugar and of rum, with bits and bridles, saddles, powder, and all the usual items of a Brazilian store, in the ledger, and no doubt balanced his accounts to the last copper fraction of a milrei,* or even a testoon.

He stayed but little in Sobral, and went on to another place called Campo Grande.   From thence he passed on to Ipú, another little town in the Sertão of Ceará.   There he acted as a lawyer's clerk, but did not stay long in the place.   He had the opportunity of entering into politics in Ipú, as his employers were agents for one of the parties who aspired, as parties do both in Brazil and in Great Britain, to be the saviours of the State.

At this time, however, Antonio Maciel, not yet advanced to the dignity of " Conselheiro," seems to have been more anxious about the welfare of his own soul than of the welfare of the body politic.   Instant in church and at confession, he seems to have been an ardent Catholic.

* Milrei, literally 1,000 reis.   The coin equals a dollar, more or less.   The first time that a bill is handed you in reis, it takes the breath away, for it may easily run to several thousands, and the receiver of it wonders if his bank account can stand the strain of it. It has its compensation in the feeling of magnificence it superinduces, just as one feels richer after reading of a lakh of rupees.

In Ipú he received the blow that altered all his way of life, and in the end led him into the paths that made him celebrated. His wife, who, as a chronicler of his life and miracles opines, had hitherto been content with besmirching his household gods,* now left these Lares once for all behind her and went off with an officer of the police.

Antonio Maciel, who was above all things honest and regular in his life, was overwhelmed with shame. It may be that the dishonest action of the Paphian police official inspired him with distrust of law and order as a whole ; but from that time, at any rate, his outlook on the world was altered and his whole life was changed.

His first idea was to hide his head where he was quite unknown, so he went off to the south of Ceará. There fate, in a place called Pãos Brancos, threw him in the way of the disturber of his household peace. Not recognising that the seducer of his wife had done him a great service in taking off with him a woman who, in the speech of the Sertão, was common as the hens, the blood of his wild family boiled up in his veins. The careful store-keeper, the approved communicant, became, for the first and last time in his life, a true descendant of the fierce partisans whose exploits terminated with the grim death of Miguel Carlos Maciel. Not able to put his hand on the seducer, he lay wait by night for a relation who had sheltered him, attacking him with all the fury of a jaguar robbed of its whelps. The victim of the assault, at the trial of Antonio Maciel, did all he could to save

* " Manchó seus Lares," Euclydes da Cunha os Sertãos.

him, alleging that the injured husband was quite within his rights. This sign of grace so character-istic of a primitive, recognised that the motive, not the mere action, is what really matters in a deed of any kind—at least to theologians—and in a way places the simple dwellers in the Sertão far above men who walk surrounded by the trammels of the town, and can see nothing but results.

His generosity did not save Antonio Maciel, who was consigned to prison on the spot. Prisons in country districts of Brazil, and generally of South America, are not the places that we know in Europe, brutally bare, silent and soul-breaking, but partake more of the Oriental pattern, wherein the prisoner lies in chains and filth, but can still talk and see his friends when they appear to bring him food. The European prison kills the soul, the dungeon in the East leaves the soul free, but breaks the body, and so mankind is justified of works.

Not seldom, in the Americas, the gaol is built of sun-baked bricks, easily pierced through with a knife. The prisoners, unlike their Eastern colleagues, are seldom chained or bound, and thus escapes are frequent, and are often looked upon as a relief by those who have to guard the malefactors. Antonio Maciel was not for long an inmate of the " calaboose,"* but soon escaped, and after being recognised upon the road to a place called Crato, finally disappeared, and left no trace of his existence in the world of the Sertão.

Ten years had passed, and the quiet cashier and outraged husband was as forgotten as if he had been

* Calabouço.

ANTONIO CONSELHEIRO   67

bound to shrivel up in the dry soil of the Sertão. He
vanished as completely as a stone sinks out of sight in
the pitch lake of Trinidad.

Nature in Brazil is so tremendous, not cut in
squares and utterly subdued and tamed as here in
Europe ; it is so overpowering in its strength that it
reduces man to the proportions of an ant, busy, but
futile in his enterprises against her immensity. A house
decays and falls, and in a year or two the house itself
and the few cultivated fields around it, wrung from the
jungle with fire and axe and hoe, have disappeared.
Over them waves a secondary jungle, swallowing
them up, and in the course of time turning once more
to the primeval forest, as if the force of Nature scorned
the puny efforts of mankind.

When a man dies he, too, is soon forgotten. His
children scarce remember him, and their children, if
they have heard of him at all, seem to regard him as
an entity that lived a thousand years ago. Life,
Nature and the vastness of the country, all give this attitude ; and so Antonio Maciel was quite forgotten, and
the churches in the little towns, where he had prayed
and knelt before the images of saints in ecstasy, knew
him no more. Public opinion naturally concerned
itself but little with a man who owed no lives,* and
whose one poor excursion in the footsteps of his clan
had proved infructuous.

What he was doing, how he lived during these ten
veiled years, that is to us unknown. Perhaps, like
another John the Baptist, he retired into the desert,
that forcing ground of saints. He may have lived

* To owe a life is to have killed a man. The debt is due to God.

amongst the Indians.   He himself never once unlocked his lips upon his wanderings.   Years afterwards, when he was dead and gone, a faithful follower, an old " Caboclo " confessed to having seen him at rare intervals wandering about and wrapped in silence, answering but by a gesture or a word to those who spoke to him.

At any rate, after ten years, he one day reappeared in the State of Bahia, but wonderfully changed.   The smug cashier, dressed carefully in white drill and clean straw hat, had vanished, and in his place Antonio Maciel appeared—an anchorite.   Sunburned and worn with fasting, his eyes wide open, fixed and staring, his sunken face, and his thin limbs, worn with privation, gave him the look of a monk from the Thebais. He wore no hat, and his long hair fell on his shoulders.   His beard was rough and spread out on his chest, uncombed and biblical.   His dress was a long shirt of coarse, blue linen, and he leaned upon the classic pilgrim's staff, knotted and gnarled, but shiny with long use.

Silent and unapproachable, he must have looked a little like a Moorish saint, sitting before a Mosque. He was not mad, and yet not altogether sane, but probably just on that borderland in which dwell saints and visionaries, and all those folk who feel they have a mission to declare, a world to save, and a vague Deity they have to glorify.

CHAPTER III

In the striking phrase of Euclydes da Cunha, his chief biographer, Antonio Maciel had become " an old man of thirty."*

His life was calculated to make him well known to all in the Sertão, where news from the outside world is rare, and where men's interest concentrates on local matters; just as in the East a wandering saint draws more attention to himself than the news of some great event abroad excites a market-place or fair.

All is in the point of view. To some, battles and sieges, and to others material progress by the way of aeroplane, of submarine and telephone, appear the chiefest objects of man's contemplation in this transitory life. To some it is a matter of the soul, for they perceive that, after all, material progress often leaves a man a mere barbarian, self-satisfied and dull.

So in the Sertão the fame of Antonio Mendes Maciel grew and extended. His very semi-madness gave him authority, marking him out as one in closer contact with the Deity than ordinary men. Thus, in the East, the actions of a madman are condoned and disappear in the holiness that madness wraps him in and separates him from the mere rational crowd com-

* " Um velho de treinta annos."

petent to buy and sell, to fight, intrigue, and chaffer,
but doomed for ever, by their very sanity itself, to
tread material ways.

About this time his name was merged in that of
Conselheiro, for he advised the country people as to
their religious duties, intervened in their disputes, and
thus became a personage throughout the district and
far beyond its bounds.

From the Sertão of Pernambuco he passed on to
Sergipe, arriving at the town of Itabariana in the year
1874. There he was quite unknown ; but the appari-
tion in the streets of the strange figure of the hermit
soon made a deep impression on the inhabitants.

Along the sandy streets, which as in most Brazilian
country towns are like the beds of dried-up brooks in
summer, torrents in winter, he wandered silently. He
never spoke unless he was addressed, and his appearance certainly must have been both strange and striking as he wandered up and down. His long, blue
gown, without a belt, made him look even thinner
than he was and more emaciated. His pilgrim's hat,
which he wore generally hanging upon his shoulders,
after the fashion of a Thessalian shepherd in classic
times, his sandalled feet, and his wide-open staring*
eyes, gave him the look as of a mad Messiah of the
Oriental type. In a hide bag which dangled by his
side, he carried paper, ink and pens, a Missal, and a
Book of Hours.†

He lived entirely upon alms, rejecting all but just
sufficient for his daily sustenance. Rarely he slept
beneath a roof, but made his bed upon a board out in

---

* Olhos fulgurantes.   † " As Horas Mariannas."

the open air, or on the ground itself. His silence, his long hair and beard, his abstinence, and the complete and absolute innocence of his life, soon made him looked upon, if not exactly as a saint, still as a man removed from sin and with a mission to fulfil. On the high pavements round the houses, at the corners of the streets, where in Brazil in country towns men congregate, their horses tied to the dark, hard-wood posts set for that purpose at almost every door, the Sertanejos lowered their voices when he passed, muttering, "There goes the Councillor."

In a society, such as that of the Sertão in the year 1874, where men believed in the snake charmers known as Mandingueiros,* in the efficacy of the Green Beads ("as Contas Verdes") brought from Africa, which made the wearer of a necklace invulnerable to bullet and to knife, a man such as Antonio Conselheiro soon rose to eminence. Nothing was talked of but his sanctity. Legends began to grow about the cures he wrought in cases given over by ordinary practitioners as quite desperate. The manner of his wanderings was changed. No longer did he stray about like a lost hound of heaven, seeking for crusts at the roadside. Followers had come to him quite unsolicited. Women of course flocked to the invisible standard that they perceived he had unfurled, as they have always flocked to any visionary. Their happiness was to endure all that their Christ endured. To live on alms, to sleep out in the open air, to bear the whips

* The name is taken from the African tribe of the Mandingos. In the days of slavery, amongst the other slaves, Ju-Ju and Gri-Gri men had been brought over, and these continued their rites and superstitions in Brazil.

and stings of fools, to have the finger pointed at them, as in their rags they passed along the streets, tickled their vanity, ministered to their pride of faith, or really aroused a spirit of devotion and self-sacrifice.

Who shall sound all the mysteries of the human heart, or put his finger on the motives that influence mankind ? Humble in purple, swollen with pride in rags ; puffed with good fortune, or steadfast against all the whirligigs of fate : by turns a bar of iron or a weathercock—each man is, has been, and will ever be, a mystery to his fellow-slaves chained to this moving sphere. The followers who flocked to Conselheiro were of the usual kind who at first flock to prophets when they first begin to preach. Herdsmen and paddlers of canoes, shepherds and fishermen, always the first to rally to a Messiah of any kind, broken to faith and patience as are the followers of either calling, formed his first converts or his sectaries. Outcasts, negroes, those dwellers in the two-fold Bohemia of poverty and colour, left the begging bowl or the scythe lying in the swathe, and swelled the rout of the faithful, to which was added a due leavening of thieves and of those men who in wild regions such as the Sertão begin their life with a yoke of oxen, which gradually produce a herd. The men who kill their neighbours' cattle under the shelter of the darkness, and sell the hide with the distinguishing brand cut out, came on their thin, ill-fed, indomitable horses, and formed a guard of rustic cavalry. All these folk, defeated in the strife of life, were just the kind of men to rally to a prophet, even though he did not preach, for at this time there is no evidence that Antonio

Conselheiro had begun that series of pronouncements against both the civil and the religious government which made him famous and eventually cost him his life.

In a country such as Brazil, where the elementary necessaries of life are easily obtained, and in which everybody in the Sertão, at least, lives upon horseback, frequently sleeps out in the open air, and all fare frugally, such an existence, intolerable to Europeans, to them was bearable enough. The prophet seems to have had no settled object in his wanderings, but roamed about from town to town, village to village, and from camping ground to camping ground, just as the spirit moved him and the whim of the moment operated.

His following was ever growing. Vaqueiros, dressed in leather, armed at all points with blunderbuss and a sword stuck underneath their saddle girth, the long sharp " faca da ponta,"* the " jacaré " or " parnahyba " in their belts, and now and then a pair of rusty pistols with flint-locks, formed, as it were, the aristocracy of the new prophet's following. The bulk of it was composed of half-castes, mulattoes, negroes, even " Caboclos,"† and the strange, simian-looking half-breeds betwixt the Indian and the negro known as Cafuces in Brazil.

He neither asked for nor rejected followers. Prostitutes, women who had deserted husbands and children to follow after God, others with little ones following at their heels as a foal follows a brood mare,

* All these are names for different kinds of knives.
† Tame Indians.

even an occasional Tapuya* who had left the woods at the fame of Antonio Conselheiro, made up the motley rout. Two of his neophytes carried with them a little altar made of cedar-wood. In it was placed a rudely sculptured Christ, before whom all the faithful knelt at the crossings of the roads where it was hung upon a tree for them to see and to adore.

They threw themselves upon the ground, beat on their breasts, confessed their sins in public; then, pure, and relieved of the black burden which the accumulated evil deeds of years had made intolerable, resumed the tenor of their lives, and once again began to lay up matter for a new general confession and a fresh start in sin.† At their approach to any town or village they bore the altar at the head of the procession, and after it followed the company, all singing hymns.

Antonio Conselheiro at this time seems not to have assumed the functions of a leader. He merely followed his ordinary life, wandering about from town to town with an ever-growing multitude accompanying his steps. In no other country of the world, out of the East, could such a strange phenomenon have been observed. In North America, the home of

---

* This is the generic name given to wild Indians.

† The portable altar was nothing new in Brazil. Henry Koster, in his excellent and interesting "Travels in Brazil" (London, 1817), has a curious description of how certain priests, with a licence from their bishop, used to travel round the State of Pernambuco with a little altar on a pack-saddle, saying mass at the different farmhouses, marrying couples who had not had the opportunity of being legally blessed, and christening children. In my youth, I remember the periodical visits of a bishop in the Province of Entre Rios for the same purpose. He travelled in a carriage, and the more illiterate Gauchos were divided in opinion as to whether he was the "Holy Father" or the "Eternal Father" himself.

strange and millenary sects, even Joseph Smith, the Prophet of Nauvoo, had never wandered with his Mormon followers about the towns of the United States. When forced to leave Nauvoo, the Mormons went off straight into the desert to found a Zion there, where they could live quite uncontaminated by the presence of the infidel. Nothing was further from Antonio Conselheiro's mind. If he had wished to shake the dust from off his sandalled feet of the comparatively slight civilisation in which he moved, nothing could have been easier. The Vaqueiros only had to drive their cattle further west, and in a week at most lands would have been reached at least as fertile as the lands of the Sertão. There he could have set his Ebenezer up, cleared farms from the primeval forest, and gone on living undisturbed by Government. Either this never came into his head, or possibly he felt rather than actually knew that colonies set up beyond the frontiers are doomed to failure, or to be absorbed in the waves of advancing progress, civilisation, or by whatever name you like to call the thing. Most probably he had no fixed ideas at all on any subject at that time, and was driven to act as he did subsequently by the force of circumstances.

In 1876 he entered the little town of Itapicurú de Cima with all his following. By this time his fame was growing and his name was beginning to be known outside of the Sertão. In 1887 a description of him as he appeared to ordinary eyes was printed in a journal of Rio de Janeiro called the *Folhinha Laemmert.* "There has appeared" (the journal said) " in the Sertoẽs of the north a man known as Antonio

Conselheiro, who exercises a great influence upon the people of those parts. This is due to his mysterious appearance, and ascetic habits, by means of which he imposes on their simplicity and ignorance. His hair and beard are long and wild, he wears a tunic of blue cotton, fasts often and so rigorously that he looks like a mummy. Accompanied by two female disciples ["duas professas"], his life is given up to singing hymns and litanies. He preaches and gives advice to the crowds that follow him, where the parish priests allow him to hold forth. . . . He seems intelligent, but has little education."

All this was true, and it is moreover the first definite account that is preserved of him, outside the bounds of the Sertão. Moreover, it shows that he had advanced a step upon his mission, for, for the first time, there is evidence that he had broken silence and begun to preach to his adepts. This was inevitable. A prophet who is dumb may gather fame, but hardly followers. Not that it is not easier far to talk than to refrain from talking, as parliaments can show, where many well-reputed men have lost their reputation by disregarding good occasions to keep silent, and belching forth a speech. The little town of Itapicurú de Cima was the turning-point in his career. Up to that time the loosely constituted Government had looked upon him with indifference. So many prophets had risen up in the Sertão, blethered a little (to use a Scotticism), and then fallen back into their well-earned obscurity, that Antonio Conselheiro had seemed but one of them—a star that, after twinkling for a brief space, would shortly disappear. Most Governments work in a mysterious way, performing

such small wonders as fall within their power, either
by violence or fraud.   The Government of the Sertão,
which had its seat in the town of Bahia, chose the latter
course, and as Antonio Conselheiro was getting to be
feared, brought a false charge against him. In the same
year (1876-1877), to the amazement of his followers,
who knew the innocence of his life and customs, he
was arrested suddenly and brought before a judge.
His followers wished to defend him, for they were
numerous and armed.   He at once assumed the attitude from which he never once departed during the
remainder of his life, that of a martyr and a stoic,
bearing the ills of life and man's injustice with indifference.   Bidding his followers to refrain from
violence, he gave himself up into the hands of the
authorities without resistance, and quietly went down
with them to Bahia, to meet the charge against him.

He had need of all his stoicism on the way, which
to the discredit of his escort was a veritable Via Crucis
to the man already weakened by long fastings and by
penances.   Although the soldiers beat him cruelly
upon the journey, he did not make the least complaint
of them when he arrived before his judge, wrapping
himself in the stoicism of the Indian race from which
no doubt he was descended in a more or less degree.

One thing alone disturbed him.   On arriving at
the port where he was to embark, he asked not to be
exposed to public curiosity, a boon he was entitled to
by every maxim both of humanity and of the thing
called justice, for as yet he was untried.

Arraigned before the court, he had to listen to an unjust and monstrous accusation trumped up to ruin him.
Founded upon his former troubles with his wife, he had

to meet a charge of having murdered her and at the same time killed his own mother who was sleeping by her side.   It was alleged that, being warned, a man had been seen by the neighbours to enter by a window to his wife's bedroom, that he had stolen up silently one night and fired upon the bed without first ascertaining who was there, and that the occupant had proved to be his mother, who for some reason or another was sleeping in the house.

This charge he had no difficulty in meeting, for both his mother and his wife were living ; so the authorities were forced to set him free.   Silently he left the court, and in a month or two he reappeared amongst his followers, who had been waiting for him, and now received him in the same spirit that a band of Christians of the early Church would have received one of their leaders who had been liberated after an unjust charge in Rome under the Cæsars.

Nothing was wanting but the halo that persecution gives a man ; thus the authorities by their unjust and foolish conduct had changed the wandering ascetic into a martyr, and from that time his legend grew, and his fame was assured.

His influence was doubled, and it was whispered that he had worked a miracle before his judges, and left them in the same state as Pontius Pilate, inquiring " What is truth ? "

He laid no claim to supernatural powers, nor yet denied them ; but left his followers to spread the truth according as they saw it, after the fashion of a judicious prophet, or of a man superior to men and all their frailties.

CHAPTER IV

His reappearance in the Sertão was the signal for a great outburst of rejoicing amongst his followers. In the town of Chorrochó he passed between a serried rank of his adorers wild with enthusiasm, but he himself unmoved, his eyes wide open, fixed on vacancy. His long, blue tunic gave him a look of walking in a shroud; his beard, which had grown almost to his waist in his confinement, an air as of a saint in an old picture.

The "faithful" women pressed to kiss his hand and clothes, crossing themselves as if he really had been canonised. He took it all, just as he suffered rain and sun, hunger and blows, the unjust accusations and all the other miseries of life, in the same silence which he had maintained before the judge and his accusers in the court.

In Chorrochó he lodged, or harboured, under a tree outside the little town. A chapel built near it still marks his residence. The tree itself has become sacred, its leaves a panacea for any illness throughout the countryside and to the pilgrims who frequent the place.

From that time (1878) commenced the series of miracles that the inhabitants of the Sertão attributed to him. Whether he was a party to them is undecided, for he himself neither accepted nor denied the powers he was reputed to possess. At any rate, during the next ten years he wandered up and down, in Alagoinhas, Inhambuhe, Bom Conselho, Cumbe, Pombal, and Monte Santo, all little towns or villages, with a following always increasing like an avalanche.

In all of them he left some traces of his passage, here raising the walls and gate of some old cemetery which had been left to ruin, and there repairing an old church or oratory. Sometimes, after his sermons, which, report said, were delivered with a fervour and conviction quite apostolic in their zeal, the rude Vaqueiros would collect funds to build a chapel or a church. Most of these still remain to witness to his fame and the devotion of his followers.

In 1887 he appeared upon the coast at Villa do Conde and was received by a great concourse, for his fame had gone before him from the woods of the Sertão. Into the little coast town he made his entry, not now with one poor little altar, but with flags and banners, and the population bearing the statues and the pictures of the saints taken out from the parish church to swell the ceremony. For several days the town was crowded as if a fair were going on, and the despised and persecuted sectary found himself in the position of dictator, having thrown all the local magistrates into the shade.

His followers built booths in the central square, and so great was the crowd when it was known he was about to preach, that all the converging streets were strictly barricaded. A pulpit was erected, and according to eye-witnesses his gift of speech was wonderful and its effect upon his hearers no less wonderful. His style was barbarous, and his discourse full of citations from the " Horas Mariannas," abstruse and intricate, a mixture of advice to his followers with proverbs and familiar phrases mixed with bursts of eloquence.

He spoke at length, with his eyes fixed upon the ground, with little gesture, his discourse a monotone, quieting and provocative of sleep. His hearers hung their heads, with half-closed eyes, just as the horses fastened outside the barricades hung down their heads and dozed. Then in an instant the man became transfigured. He raised his head and words streamed from his lips, so fast his hearers scarce could follow them. Prophecies, denunciations, vague threats and hints succeeded one another, and his black, sparkling eyes became so terrible that his followers dared not look at him, and turned away their heads. A sob ran through his audience and a hysteric movement, which found vent in broken phrases of " Jesus," "Ave Maria," and " Viva, O Conselheiro !" shook the assembled crowd.

Then it was, a cynical eye-witness has recorded, that he performed his real miracle, to rise above surroundings almost ridiculous, and to become inspired. So must the Gnostics and the early Christians have preached to their followers and with the like results. In their case the enemy was Paganism and still more the differences between the approaching, but slightly separated sects, a phenomenon to be observed down to the present day, when the friend who will not go with you as far as you are going is a worse foe than is the common enemy of both.

In the case of Antonio Conselheiro the enemy was

the Church, fallen, as he saw her, from her proud estate, and sore in need of a thorough reformation from within, of which the prophet was to be the instrument. Quite naturally the preaching friars, of whom a considerable store existed in Brazil, were all his enemies. He poached upon their province, drew from the country people the contributions that they had looked upon as their own privilege, and quite outdid them in the sphere of preaching which they considered their especial territory in the religious field. The doctrines and the morality that Antonio Conselheiro preached were singularly like those enunciated by Montanus or by the Carpocratians in the second century. Antonio Conselheiro enjoined an exaggerated chastity, thundering against marriage, and threatening with all the pains of hell women who adorned their persons, dressed their hair or made themselves desirable in any way to men. Those who continued to wear combs had crowns of thorns put on their heads instead, to curb their vanity. Beauty itself was an anathema sent upon earth by Satan for the undoing of mankind. Antonio himself exhibited an affected horror of it. He never looked a woman in the face when speaking to her, carrying his precautions to the same length even when talking to the old " beatas,"* who, as a contemporary Brazilian writer says, were fitted more to daunt a satyr than to excite concupiscence in any ordinary man.

The doctrines that Antonio Conselheiro preached in

---

* A " beata," in Spanish and Portuguese, infers a woman given up to religious ceremonies and church-going. She is always dressed in black clothes that smell of incense.

the Sertão had an extraordinary likeness to those advanced by several of the Gnostic sectaries, the same blind terror of the power of Antichrist, who was to reign on earth, turning all to confusion and setting up an empire of unreason and of blood—as if it wanted any Antichrist to bring about such a condition of affairs in an unreasonable world. The faithful were enjoined to abandon all their possessions in the face of the impending final judgment, which was awaited confidently and without escape. Meanwhile they were to give all they had in to the common treasury—for, by degrees, Antonio Conselheiro, though quite disinterested, foresaw the time when he would have to withdraw himself and all his followers into some stronghold, where the world could not defile nor influence his flock.

This millenarianism, curiously enough, in the face of all his preaching chastity and the duty of not continuing the race by breeding sinners to be damned eternally, furthered the practice of free love. It mattered little what men did as the world was to last so short a time, and thus salvation was assured by faith, without the mere formality of works.

In writing of the Gnostics of the second century, Irenæus said : " They hold man shall not be saved by mere good works, but by his spiritual nature, which is incapable of corruption, whatever they may do ; just as clay cannot injure gold, so their spiritual nature cannot be lost by any kind of conduct."*

Most certainly the rude sectaries of the Sertão had

* Irenæus I., III. ff. 1. These doctrines were held also by the Valentinians and Simonians.

never reasoned out the matter, but merely followed out the indication of the natural theologians of every race and age, who, finding works a task too onerous for " their conversing," fly for relief to faith.

Antonio Conselheiro, though an unconscious Gnostic, could have known nothing of the Sophia, or held the belief that the principle of thought was male and female at the same time, as did so many of the Gnostic sects. Still less could he have heard anything about the Seven Worlds, dear to so many of the primitives; but all the same, judged by his preaching and the effect it had upon his followers, he was an unconscious Montanist, or perhaps a Carpocratian, preserved miraculously, just as a mammoth is occasionally found preserved in ice, in the Siberian wilds. Nature, it would appear, is indestructible, preserving prehistoric forms and follies intact for us to wonder at, to imitate and copy, and to perpetuate, so that no form of man's ineptitude shall ever perish, or be rendered unavailable for fools to promulgate. Antonio's precepts were that his followers should renounce all happiness here in this transitory world. No doubt the " beatas " and the more spiritual of his followers attempted to act up to what he preached, but many of the vagabonds who flocked to his tattered standard looked at things from another point of view, giving themselves up, as did the Carpocratians of old, to unrestricted fornication (" devant le seigneur ") and to drunkenness.

All principles to which men turn for assistance in their struggle with their lives seem greatly fallacious. Faith often leads straight to fanaticism, and to a disregard of works, plunging its votaries into an abyss of self-absorption, leaving their brethren starving in the mire whilst the believer saves his miserable soul. Good works, pursued for their own sake alone, induce arrogance and a self-satisfaction that shrivels up the soul. Logic remains ; but then, again, the followers of Antonio Conselheiro who engaged in pious orgies were surely logical enough, for if the world is to end directly, it is best to get what we can out of it, whilst our life still remains.

When faith and works, philosophy, logic, and the rest of the panaceas that have been preached, accepted, and been found wanting during the past two thousand years or so, have failed, all that is left to reasonable men is to pay bootmakers' and tailors' bills with regularity, give alms to the deserving and to the undeserving poor, and then live humbly underneath the sun, taking example by the other animals.

When the gift of prophecy has descended on a man, he can as little hide its light under a bushel as one can hide a cough, or love, or as a minor poet can refrain from troubling the public with titubating lines.

Antonio Conselheiro was no exception to the rule, and he announced several years of misfortune to lead up to the destruction of the world.

" In 1896," he said, " a multitude shall come up from the shore to the Sertão. The Sertão shall then become a sea-beach and the shore become Sertão. In 1898 there shall be many hats and a great scarcity of heads. In 1899 the waters shall be all changed to blood and a planet shall appear in the East . . . a great fall of stars shall bring about the destruction of the world. In 1900 all lights shall be extinguished.

God says in his Holy Gospel 'I will have but one fold and one shepherd . . . for I have but a single flock.'"

These prophecies, which the declarer of them did not live long enough to see confirmed, were found after his death in the mystic city of Canudos that he founded, written on scraps of paper and old pocket-books. They were what may be styled "terre à terre" prophecies, common to every vulgar self-ordained mystery-monger the whole world over, from the first dawn of Christianity.

Antonio Conselheiro sometimes rose to greater heights and became interesting by the extravagance of his beliefs, and by the fervour of his faith. One of his sermons is remarkable. " In the ninth hour, resting upon the Mount of Olives, one of His apostles asked our Lord . . . ' Lord, what sign wilt Thou give us, so that we may be ready for the destruction of the world ?' He answered them . . . ' Many signs in the Moon, the Sun, and in the Stars. An angel shall appear, sent by My Father. He shall preach at every door and shall establish cities in the desert, churches and chapels, and shall give council unto men.' " After the fashion of the Gnostics, he seems to have considered himself one with Christ, confounding, as it were, the persons, and the essences of each, into one body and one soul. So did the Gnostic preachers of the second century in their ecstasies. Montanus held that the prophet is a lyre to transmit the precepts of the Deity. Thus all his prophecies were delivered during ecstasy, a fact that the shrewd Irenæus was not slow to seize upon. "True prophets," all the orthodox averred, delivered their *charisma* after ecstasy. Therefore the utterances of Montanus were not those of the Divinity.

The point is a nice one, and would seem to apply not only to Montanus, but to Antonio Conselheiro; his unconscious fellow-theologians will perceive at once that neither Montanus nor Antonio Conselheiro were true ecstatics; or, at least, their prophecies not having been digested, as it were, they were mere journalists of prophecy, writing of current matters as do journalists, and not as artists, after the events had become clarified by time. In fact, they fell into the category of paræsthetics, a trifling set of whom the world has always been quite worthy, just as they were worthy of the world.

This did not hinder the followers both of Montanus and of Antonio Conselheiro from taking their utterances as the *ipsissima verba* of the Deity, although we know that this could not have been the case.

Both prophets had one circumstance attaching to their lives, that made their likeness still more striking, for both of them were joined by two female adepts who had left their husbands to follow after truth. The coadjutors of Montanus were named Maximilla and Priscilla; those of Antonio Conselheiro have not had their names preserved. In neither case does the least breath of scandal tarnish their memories.

Although Antonio Conselheiro held the doctrine of faith in its entirety, his practice was better than his belief, and, in the intervals between his sermons and his prophecies, he yet had time for works. All over the Sertão he wandered, with a crowd of carpenters and masons following him, who worked for nothing,

building and renovating churches, chapels, and cemeteries. His flock gave stone and wood and all the
requisites for work, free, without charge of any kind,
hoping perhaps to receive their reward in heaven, or,
perhaps, from real charity and kindness, seeking no
payment, either in this world or the next. All the
time that the work was going on, those who were
not employed in carrying wood or stones sang hymns ;
their leader sat on a log of wood or on the ground,
acting as overseer.

A man who saw him at this date* (1887) describes
him as " short, dark, and Indian-looking (acaboclado),
with long hair and beard."   He says he lived at that
time in an unfurnished house to which the " beatas "
brought provisions, and waited on him.   The kind of
life he led and the part that he took in spiritual affairs,
such as baptisms, feasts, novenas, and the like, aroused
the jealousy both of the preaching friars and of the
regular clergy, who found their reserves attacked by
the unauthorised ministrations of Antonio Conselheiro
and his excursions into a field peculiarly their own.
They flew to arms, and looked at him, not without
reason, just as a blackleg is regarded by a trade
unionist.   Already, in the year 1882, the Archbishop
of Bahia had sent a circular throughout his diocese to
all the parish priests, in which he said : " It having
come to my notice that one Antonio Conselheiro has
begun preaching to the people, exhorting them to an
excessively rigid morality,† thus troubling men's con-

* Lieut.-Colonel Darval Vieira de Aguiar, " Descripcoes practicas
da provincia da Bahia."
† " Un moral excessiuamente rigida."

sciences, and weakening the authority of the priest-hood, we call upon you to prohibit all your flock from listening to the preaching of this man." The Arch-bishop does not seem to have been too happy in the composition of his pastoral. Rigid morality was not a drug in the Sertão, and a mere layman might have thought that the best way to combat such exhortations would have been to spur the priesthood on to a like cause themselves, instead of silencing the interloper.

All the Archbishop's efforts were infructuous. The people still flocked to the preaching of the prophet, bringing their offerings ; and though there is no evidence that their morality was in the least improved, the churches all through the district were deserted and left desolate.

The terrors of the Church having been of no avail, the secular arm next stepped into the breach. The authorities of Itapicurú wrote (in the year 1886) to the chief of police in Bahia to the following effect.

After informing the head of the police that Antonio Conselheiro was camped close to the town, followed by hundreds of persons of both sexes, he went on to say : "The fanaticism of his followers knows no bounds. It is certain that a chapel has been built, a thing most necessary, at the expense of the town, but the sacrifice is greater than the benefit received, for all Antonio Conselheiro's followers flock to his ministra-tions, leaving the vicar without a congregation in his church. . . . The fanatics look up to their leader as if he were a god . . . almost a living god. Often more than a thousand persons come to hear him preach." In regions such as the Sertão, where distances are great and roads are non-existent, this was an enormous gathering, for the faithful probably came from many miles away. The " authority" went on to say : "The chapel cost about a hundred thousand reis, and all the workmen are from Ceará. These, as his countrymen, Antonio Conselheiro blindly protects, allowing them to commit all sorts of disorders, so that they go on with their work. . . . A dispute having arisen between the fanatics and the Vicar of Inhambupé, both sides armed themselves as for a battle, and the peaceful inhabitants were terrified to see the sectaries equipped with blunderbusses, swords and knives, and making ready to attack."

The expected battle seems not to have taken place. Perhaps the vicar's followers were as well armed as were the sectaries : for nothing further is recorded of the matter by the " authority " of Itapicurú.

In 1887 the Archbishop of Bahia once more intervened, this time on the petition of the clergy of the diocese, who informed him that the " cause of our holy faith is suffering, through the proceedings of one Antonio Maciel, who is trying to convince the people that he is the Holy Ghost."

Either Antonio Conselheiro was proving more ambitious in his claims, or, as is probable, the clergy had misrepresented him, for he himself does not appear to have advanced pretensions of the kind or to have said that he was other than an ordinary man who had a mission to fulfil.

The Archbishop wrote to the Governor of the province upon the matter, and he wrote to a minister of state, saying a madman had arisen in the

Sertão who seemed as if he might give trouble, and asked if there was a cell vacant in the " Hospicio de Alienados " at the capital, in which the madman could be placed. The minister replied that there was no cell vacant—an admirable answer and a diplomatic, worthy of any state department—and no doubt pigeon-holed the correspondence, after the fashion of his kind. Nothing was done, and the plan of the Governor of Bahia, who seems to have been the only reasonable man who intervened in the mad business, was forgotten, and the fame of Antonio Conselheiro grew enormously. Legends began to cluster round about his doings, and reputable witnesses averred, as they have continuously averred in the like cases since the world began, that they had seen him work his miracles.

In Bom Jesus, when ten stout workmen were endeavouring to raise a beam, the prophet told them to desist, and pointing with his finger to two, and those not the most robust of them, he ordered them to lift the burden, a task which they accomplished easily. This was seen by good Catholics who were certain that they were not deceived. Thought transference is a commonplace phenomenon; but transference of force is not so common, and it is reassuring to reflect that both the witnesses to it were regular communicants and had complied with all the ordinances.

Another time the prophet came to Monte Santo and ordained that there should be a great procession to the highest chapel on the hill. Like a long snake the multitude wound its way up the mountain upon the path cut in the solid rock. It stopped to pray at all

the oratories. The heat was terrible, and many of
the faithful faltered and fell out by the way. At the
head of the procession marched Antonio Conselheiro,
silent and corpse-like, his body worn by penitences,
and his soul disturbed by its continual yearnings for
union with his God.

Night fell upon the multitude as they toiled
upwards, and the line of torches which they held must
have appeared to people in the plains below like a
long file of glow-worms slowly advancing through the
gloom. At last they reached the highest chapel on
the rock. There Conselheiro sat himself down upon a
boulder and fell into an ecstasy. Long did he gaze
upon the heavens, watching the stars as they appeared
like fire-flies in the deep-blue of the calm, tropic night
above his head. Meantime the faithful waited, seated
on the rocks, silent and wondering. Passing amongst
the throng that opened as he advanced, he went into
the chapel, his eyes bent down upon the earth.
Before the altar he paused, raised up his head and
pointed with his finger to the most Holy Virgin,
God's Mother, who with her baby in her arms looked
down compassionately upon the exhausted multitude
who had struggled up the stony Calvary to do her
honour and to worship at her shrine. The crowd
turned towards the image, and lo ! a miracle occurred,
seen plainly by them and manifest to everyone who
stood within the fane. Two tears of blood rolled
down the holy countenance—tears of compassion,
it was said, for all the sufferings that the crowd
had undergone upon its pilgrimage. Thus through
the Sertão by degrees the prophet's fame became

established. His miracles were well attested and believed, though he himself never put forth the smallest claim to supernatural power. In all his actions he had taken care never to infringe the law, although it is evident that by degrees tension between his followers and the authorities was gradually increased. The smallest spark sufficed to light the flame and place the prophet in opposition to the law, and push him to the course which in the end led to his ruin and the death of all his followers.

CHAPTER V

As by degrees the tension between the authorities and the followers of the prophet increased and grew more serious, so did he himself assume a different air towards the world. At first he had been content with the uncomplaining martyr's rôle, accepting stripes quite apostolically, and all the slights of jacks-in-office, and of fools, without a protest or a word. Things were to alter, and one day, in a place called Natubá, the vicar was amazed at the appearance of a man, lean, lank, and worn with fasting, who asked for shelter for the night. In the Sertão hospitality is universal, and no one ever is turned away from anybody's door who asks for a night's lodging and a bed. The unusual guest refused the offer of a bed, preferring to sleep upon a board on the verandah, dressed as he was, without even taking off the raw-hide sandals that he wore upon his feet. Next morning he asked leave to preach during a festival, for a multitude of country folk had come from far and near to attend the ceremony. The vicar answered, "Only a priest is competent to preach on such occasions in the church." Then his guest demanded to be allowed to make the Via Sacra, and this too was refused. Then, drawing from his bag a cloth, he waved it in the air, and taking off his sandals, shook the dust from them before the astonished priest ; then, looking at him fixedly for a moment, he went away without a word, the crowd all making way for him as if he were a saint.

Thus did he make the apostolic protest, and for the last time act the part of a submissive martyr, content to suffer all indignities and turn the other cheek. From this time he became a different man, irascible under the smallest contradiction; a dominating personality which had been long kept under now came uppermost.

One day he reappeared again in the village of Natubá in which the vicar had affronted him.   The church was ruinous, and as it chanced the vicar was away from home upon a visit to his parishioners. Without a word, Antonio Conselheiro ordered his followers to collect material to put the church in order, and when the astonished priest returned, he found an enormous pile of stones ready for use in front of the church door, and a great crowd encamped. His fury knew no bounds, and he at once placed an embargo on the stones, saying that he would use them for a road.   This time the prophet made no silent protest ; but standing just before the porch, with arm outstretched and his eyes flaming, launched a most comprehensive curse against the vicar, his church, the village and all that dwelt in it, and then departed, followed by the multitude formed in procession singing a hymn, till they had left the accursed spot behind.

So passed away a year or two, his power always increasing, and his followers once more numerous.

Then came the abdication of the Emperor Don Pedro
de Alcantara, in the year 1893. This event naturally
changed the outlook of the Brazilian people upon
politics and life. It affected few more intimately than
Antonio Conselheiro, brought up as he had been in an
atmosphere of feudalism and of ecclesiasticism. All
his preconceived notions of authority were outraged,
and his religious instincts received a shock before the
liberal attitude of the republic. During Don Pedro's
reign, though liberal himself, things had gone on
without much alteration, partly from lack of initiative,
partly because the central authority was weak, partly
from the lack of roads, and the enormous size of the
Brazilian territory.

Things natural in themselves, that the new republic
was obliged to institute, seemed daring innovations to
the folk in the Sertão. Up to that moment (1893)
Antonio Conselheiro had limited himself to a silent
but an effective protest against the lethargy of the clergy,
and their neglect to repair their chapels and churches
when they fell into decay. From 1893 he took his
stand as a politician, raising his protest against the
Government.

The event took place in a town known as Bom
Conselho that was to bring him into conflict with the
law. Municipalities had been proclaimed autonomous,
that is to say they had the power of raising local rates
legally vested in them by a decree of the new Government.

Upon the notice-boards of Bom Conselho one day
there appeared some notice or another about taxation
or the levying of rates. Why, it does not appear, for

up to that time Antonio Conselheiro had rendered scrupulously to Cæsar what was due and undue to him ; he fell into a fury at the sight of the offending notices.

Calling the people all together after a fiery sermon, he had a bonfire lighted, and making as he said himself an " auto da fé," he burned the offending noticeboards to the accompaniment of hymns. He then proclaimed an insurrection, calling the republic the spawn of Satan, and an attempt to paganise the land. This done, he seems to have realised the gravity of his proceedings, and, followed by his flock, he took the way towards the north to give a clearer field for operations in a country still little settled and scantily populated. The Government sent all the forces they could muster in the province to capture him and to disperse his followers, and thus nip the insurrection in the bud before it gathered strength. Two hundred soldiers, ill armed and still worse officered, was all that they could lay their hands upon, and out of these only some thirty regulars were properly equipped. At a place called Massete they overtook the rebels in a little open plain. The thirty well-armed soldiers advanced upon the crowd, certain of victory. At their first fire dozens of sectaries were stretched upon the ground. Then their ranks opened and disclosed their rustic cavalry. These charged upon the soldiers, firing their blunderbusses; then falling like a thunderbolt on them, with their cattle goads and knives routed them utterly. The colonel gave the signal for the flight, setting the example by galloping away without a thought for what might happen to his men so that he saved his life.

Many were killed and the remainder saved themselves by a prompt flight into the woods. The prophet and his followers gained the first victory and remained upon the field.

From this time forward they either took the name of Jagunços,* or else it was applied to them in recognition of the prowess in their first stricken field. Their victory had the result of bringing in new followers, who flocked to the prophet's standard in such numbers that a new force of eighty soldiers sent from Bahia dared not attack them, and returned home without a fight.

In this they acted prudently, for in such districts as the Sertão, bushy and broken up by barriers of rocks, regular troops fought at a disadvantage with men brought up to frontier warfare from their youth, and all accustomed to bear arms. Thus was the die cast between Antonio Conselheiro and his proselytes, and the new republic. Though he was a mere fanatic in religious matters he was not blind as to the consequences of his rash action, even though crowned with victory at first.

He at once perceived that the republic would send larger forces to apprehend him and to disperse his followers. Though his strength had been increased by his late success—the country-people flocking to him from all sides, eager to kiss the hem of his long cotton robe, and hail him as a Christ—he saw he must withdraw farther afield to some place capable of making a defence.

Nobody better than himself knew the recesses of

* Jagunços almost equals " Bravos."   See note in Introduction.

the Sertão.   For nearly twenty years he had traversed it on foot, and there was not a fastness with which he was not well acquainted, or a mountain path he had not trodden in his pilgrimage.   Perhaps, long before his final break with the authorities, he had determined where to repair and build his Zion, when he was forced to flee farther into the more thinly peopled portion of the country, or perhaps he merely hit upon the place in his march towards the north.   At any rate, with a vast multitude he set out, steadily north-wards, his following growing like a snowball as he proceeded on his way.   At last, in the autumn of the year 1893, he reached Canudos, a spot hitherto un-known to fame.   There he determined to prepare a place fit for defence and build a city far from the haunts of men.

CHAPTER VI

In 1893, after a long and painful journey, during whose course the people marched singing hymns, and with their portable altars and rough images of saints borne in the van, the prophet reached his goal. This was an old fazenda,* fallen into ruins and abandoned to decay, known as Canudos,† a name destined to be carried far and wide through the vast territory of Brazil. Euclydes da Cunha in his "Os Sertões," the chief authority for the events which happened there and for the life and the career of Antonio Conselheiro, tells us that at the time the prophet reached it all it consisted of was but some twenty huts. An idle population, armed to the teeth, whose chief occupation lay in drinking rum and smoking home-grown tobacco in long pipes whose stems were reeds cut on the river bank, formed its inhabitants. The river was the Vasa-Barris, a considerable stream in the north of the State of Bahia, a territory larger than many a kingdom in the Old World. Throughout the vast and turbulent district, everyone went armed ; all were born horsemen, every man in a more or less degree a devout and all-believing Catholic, and in things spiritual the local vicar was supreme. Naturally, he

---

* Fazenda, cattle farm, or almost any country establishment.
† Reeds.

had scant influence upon men's actions, for they have always had, and possibly will ever have, a way of escaping from the thraldom of morality and faith. Men bow the knee and huddle up the mind into a nutshell, whilst still believing ready to persecute all those who differ from them, yet live like pagans, uninfluenced by the faith that they profess, still less by charity.

So it was with the people of the Sertões. The Vicar of Cumbé, he whom Antonio Conselheiro publicly cursed and shook the dust off from his sandals in his face, has left a record that the inhabitants of Canudos, at the time when the prophet first arrived there, were " an idle folk and given up to vice." Their miserable huts, cane-built, and thatched with leaves of cabbage palm, looking like Indian wigwams, or like " wickey-ups," were scattered here and there upon the river banks. The fazenda house was all in ruins. Only the church remained intact, and round it was grouped the greater portion of the huts. This church was destined to become, after it had been rebuilt, the rallying point of the Troy of the Jagunços—to use the graphic phrase of Euclydes da Cunha in his account of it. The river Vasa-Barris ran, like the Scamander, through a thick bed of reeds.

On every side the landscape stretched out arid and dead-looking, scorched by the sun in summer and in the winter burned up by the frost. The hills were almost bare of vegetation, and through the scanty bush that straggled on their sides, peeped the red earth, giving the country a look as if a forest fire were passing over it. In the more fertile portions of the district grew various Bromelias, as the Caroá,* out of whose fibres the inhabitants of the Sertão make ropes and hammocks and their fishing nets, the Ananas de Agulha,† and the Caatinga Branca,‡ whose hard, thorny leaves furnish a yellow dye. Here and there the Pereiro and the Icó flourished in spite of drought ; curious little trees that stand the heat and cold of the Sertão better than any others known, and, though innocuous to the herds of both wild cattle and of horses, are said to be a poison to a horse heated with travelling or to domesticated§ beasts.

To this deserted centre, shut in by mountains from the world, Antonio Conselheiro evidently thought that the accursed Government of the republic would never penetrate. Though it was situated not much more than two hundred miles from the town of Bahia, it was cut off from the outer world by forests, mountains, and by the lack of roads. The only railway finished at Queimadas, seventy or eighty miles away. Between it and the new Zion only led cattle tracks ; in the dry season waterless, and in the rains impassable through mud.

The prophet seems to have had an inkling how strong the place was, and how defensible, or to have been advised by some old soldier in his company. From the first moment of his arrival at Canudos he displayed a feverish energy. Men saw him eagerly

---

* *Caroa Bromelia variegata.*
† *Bromelia muricata.*   ‡ *Linparen tinctorea.*
§ I have been unable to identify these trees. Their leaves are of a very bright green colour, and when all vegetation droops and the leaves fall from the other trees, they continue green and fresh-looking. The *Spondia tuberosa* has the same drought-resisting properties.

surveying the best places to dig trenches, for this was his first care. He preached incessantly, foretelling the destruction of the world, but letting it be known that those who rallied to Canudos would be saved at the last judgment, and their lives should be prolonged. One who passed near the newly founded town at that time left the following testimony :* " Districts of the surrounding region and even reaching out as far as the Sertão of Sergipe were left uninhabited, so great was the influx of men and families who flocked towards Canudos, the place Antonio Conselheiro had selected for his operations. It made one sorry to see the extraordinary quantity of cattle, horses, goats, and other things, as houses and estates all sold for less than nothing, in their anxiety to set out on the road and have some ready money in their hands to help the ' holy Councillor ' in his mad enterprise."

Inhambupé, Tucano, Cumbé, Itapicurú, Bom Conselho, Natuba, Massacará and Monte Sacro, with half a hundred other towns in Ceará, in Pernambuco, and throughout the length and breadth of the Sertão, sent their inhabitants. The few rare travellers who ventured into regions so remote returned astonished at the sights that they had seen in the deserted towns. These were left tenantless, with the doors open, and the wild animals which had come out of the woods straying at pleasure through the streets.

Over mountain trails, and labouring slowly from the villages upon the coast, came long processions, driving their flocks and herds in front of them. In their rude bullock carts were piled the children, their

* The Baron de Geremoabo.

altars, images of saints, and their scant furniture. They
wound along, toiling through forests and through
passes of the hills, all singing hymns, armed to the
teeth, and many of them, riding the active little
horses of the country, acting as foragers. When the
last turning of the painful route was past, and finally
the longed-for sanctuary appeared towards which they
had converged, fleeing the wrath so soon to descend
upon the world, they fell upon their knees. Tears
trickled down the cheeks of the Vaqueiros, who, dismounting from their beasts, threw themselves on the
ground. Tired women beat their breasts and children
whimpered, the cattle lowed, the creaking of the
ungreased wheels was stilled, and after prayer they
joined in singing hymns of joy and thankfulness.
Before them lay the land of promise, shut in by
mountains and cut off from the world, but sanctified
to them by all the sufferings they had undergone upon
their pilgrimage. Canaan was theirs at last after
their wandering, and they were safe at least for a brief
space before the judgment day. The oxen were out-
spanned, the flocks and horses driven off to feed, and
then a ring of camp-fires lighted on the hills girdled
the town with flame.

They generally passed the night in prayer and in
thanksgiving, and in the morning started out betimes
to see the " Councillor." This pious duty duly performed, their first care was to set about to run up
some sort of dwelling-place. On every side houses
were springing up as if by magic—so rapidly, they
seemed to rise out of the ground like mushrooms
after a shower of rain. Their rudimentary nature

allowed the builders to construct ten or a dozen of them every day. Each family erected its dwelling-place exactly as it liked, and where it liked, so long as there was room.

Nothing more monstrous or chaotic was ever seen than the New Zion, in which each man was a law unto himself, except so far as that he paid in all his funds towards the common stock, and looked for spiritual guidance and salvation from the impending doom threatening humanity to the Good Councillor. So houses built of reeds sprang up without streets being planned, in groups, making the most peculiar and heterogeneous assemblage of human dwelling-places, more rudimentary far than any Indian village in the woods. Thus twisting lanes were formed with angles sharp and easily defensible, which proved invaluable to the defenders of them in the strife that was to come. The little hill called " A Favella " dominated the only open space. Another, "Os Pellados," finished on a steep bank upon the River Vasa-Barris. Two streams, the Macuin and Umburanas, ran through the town and were linked up by trenches, which the prophet, with a keen eye to future possibilities, had ordered to be dug. The houses of the modern Zion were built on an invariable plan. Outside they looked a little like an ostrich nest or the rude shelters of gorillas, built all of reeds and thatched with rushes and with palm-leaves. In taking little thought of durability the builders acted logically enough. Who would be troubled to erect a Parthenon (except an artist for his own satisfaction) if it were destined to be overwhelmed as soon as it was built ?

" Inside, all of the huts had three compartments, after the fashion of the rude buildings of the Gauls in Cæsar's " Commentaries." First came a little entrance hall, then an atrium they used indifferently both as a kitchen and a dining-room. Lastly a low and heavy door gave access to the bedroom, where slept the women and the children of the family. In a dark corner of the mud-daubed wall was set an altar, which at first sight was hardly visible amidst the smoke and gloom. About it stood or hung some images of saints rudely hewn out of wood, looking like idols in a Ju-Ju house in Calabar, or in some village in the Cameroons. Figures of San Antonio like fetishes, and Blessed Virgins so hideous that they appeared like witches, kept guard upon the heathen-looking oratory. Two or three heavy stools, a chest or two of cedar-wood, or covered baskets made of rushes, and a tin candle sconce hanging from the roof formed all the furniture. There were no beds, nor any tables, for they ate squatted on the kitchen floor, and slept in hammocks, or on the ground upon their saddle gear."*

A water bucket of raw hide, known locally as a Bogo, with some rude hunting-bags, hung from pegs stuck into the mud walls, with lazos, bridles, spurs and saddlecloths. Axes and cattle goads, with a few rustic ploughs and mattocks, stood in a corner of the hut, leaning against the wall. Their arms were all the various kinds of knives in use in the Sertão, ranging from the short Faca de Ponta that they carried in their belts, to the long Parnahyba stuck beneath their saddle girths. Bayonets with wooden

* Euclydes da Cunha, "Os Sertões."

handles, kept in place by a cow's tail put on when wet and left to shrink and become hard, old swords with wooden hilts but sharp as razors, and cattle goads shaped like an antique trident, were in the hands of all. Their firearms were at least as various : old blunderbusses and wide-mouthed pistols, that they charged with anything they had, as slugs and pebbles, small shot and bits of bone ; long-barrelled fowling pieces ; and now and then a modern rifle, bought in Bahia or Pernambuco, formed their armoury.

These they kept all well cleaned and oiled, ready for instant action, for they were well aware their Zion soon would be attacked. So closely did the agglomeration of reed huts assimilate to the prevailing colour of the landscape that from a little distance off it was invisible, till their great church was built. Even when it rose high and Babylonical above the town, you might have taken it but for a mound of earth or natural eminence in the brown landscape that surrounded it.

This property of invisibility either Antonio Conselheiro or his military adviser took full advantage of, digging his trenches with their parapets bevelled down towards the ground, so that Canudos, though fortified with care, seemed open to attack.

CHAPTER VII

His trenches opened, and the ever-increasing population that had flowed into Canudos housed, or at least sheltered in their huts, Antonio Conselheiro's first care was to draw up a scheme of life for them. He was, of course, supreme, after the fashion of all prophets and democratic leaders when they have attained to power. When a man is convinced, as was Antonio Conselheiro—for without doubt he was quite honest in his faith in himself—that he is God's vicegerent upon earth, nothing more natural than he should make himself obeyed.

The intricate lanes formed by the fantastically grouped huts, the flanking hills, and above all the strong position on the river bank, secured him from a surprise attack. Seen from a little distance off, the reed-built huts and the brown earth of the embankments disappeared into the landscape, making the whole almost invisible, and difficult to bring under artillery fire. The flocks and herds of the community grazed under an armed guard of herdsmen well to the rear of the position, upon the old Fazenda lands. Water was always procurable from the various rivers that ran close to the town, and every band of pilgrims brought some store of grain with them which was placed in the common granary.

Feeling himself secure, at least for a considerable time, he set about to mould the lives of the inhabitants according to his will. Conduct he left to individual taste, setting but little store upon it, as it would seem, for faith was his chief stronghold, in a world so soon to disappear. Ninety per cent. of all their worldly goods the faithful paid into the treasury, esteeming themselves happy with the little that remained to them, for mere material needs. " Blessed are those who suffer " was the theme that he embroidered on in all his sermons to his followers. He enjoined strict fasting, giving the example in his own person, and prolonging abstinence till he was nothing but a skeleton. Most of the day had to be passed in singing hymns and litanies. Sermons were frequent and all the population had to attend them under pain of penance and of punishment.

Under this religious regimen, the simple Sertanejos became the fiercest of fanatics, and well deserved the title of Jagunços,* by which they were beginning to be known. All went about armed to the teeth, ready to do the bidding of their prophet at the least signal ; human life, never too highly valued in the Sertão, became of still less value, though it cannot be said that Antonio Conselheiro in himself was cruel or took delight in blood.

Like others of the Gnostics, he held that virtue was superfluous, as the end of the world was fast approaching ; considering it apparently a sort of vanity,

* See note in Introduction.

or, as it were, an affectation of superiority over one's fellow-men.

Anything that ennobled life here in this transitory existence savoured of impiety, and as a setting up of oneself against the Deity, who had decreed the destruction of the world. Marriage he set but little store by, as did Montanus in the second century. Though neither of them held it was but a mere licensed fornication, as did certain of the Gnostic sects, even perhaps Tertullian, Antonio Conselheiro considered it a counsel of perfection, thinking perhaps it was unnecessary to beget children into a world so soon to disappear. Free love he seems to have tolerated, or at the least made no inquiry into the conduct of his followers. They upon their part took full advantage of his tolerance, and after passing all the day either in listening to the prophet's preaching or in singing litanies, at night indulged in orgies of the same pattern as the " mystical communion " of the Carpocratians, during the Agapes. The point, of course, has been debated since the creation of the world, and still remains debatable, as to whether man best fulfils his mission by living quietly under the laws the State sets down for him, paying his debts, marrying but a single wife at the same time, and educating all his children, or by indulging in his own desires, and then washing his sins away in a Niagara of tears. The parable of the Prodigal is, of course, the strongest argument in favour of the latter course, although to some minds repentance is a mean thing at the best, especially when it leads to the penitent getting the best of both the lines of conduct that a man is

competent to tread. " Repent, and sin no more " is
a sort of moral fire insurance. No such ideas entered
the heads of the Jagunços who sang their hymns with
fervour, passed hours in church, and fornicated briskly,
drinking as much raw rum as they could come by (for
there was no fast on the drink), and waiting patiently
for the destruction of mankind.

Antonio Conselheiro dwelt often in his sermons to
his well-armed saints upon the theme of " Blessed are
the sufferers," exhorting all his hearers to avoid
comfort, good food and clothes as they would shun the
plague. Better a mortal sin, he said, than an excess of
comfort, holding, as did the monks of the Thebais, that
dirt and ignorance, idleness and maceration of the
flesh, were things more acceptable to Him who at
the same time had given reason to mankind by which
to shape their lives.

So prophets from the beginning have assumed to
know God's mind better than He Himself ; for vanity
and pride disguised in rags and misery have been their
guiding stars. Still, it was evident Antonio Conselheiro preached in good faith and all sincerity. Had
he not done so, he would have had no followers, for
let the ecstatic, mystic, revolutionary, or any other
class of men doubt of the leader's faith, they follow
him no more.

Antonio Conselheiro practised all he preached,
fasting to the point of actual starvation, sometimes
remaining hours upon his knees in ecstasy before the
rough-hewn figures of the saints, at others busying
himself with public matters—for he was priest and
king. Although an almost absolute promiscuity

reigned amongst the faithful to an incredible degree, no one has ever brought a single accusation attaching to his name in matters sexual.

His private life was pure, his house no better than the thousand other huts clustering on every side.

His food was simple, and his dress always the invariable tunic of blue cotton, belted to the waist.

His tolerance or cynicism—for in some religious leaders it is not easy to distinguish accurately between them—at least for the lay mind—was all-embracing. On one occasion a complaint was brought to him that a Jagunço in an excess of pious fervour had seduced a girl of tender years. He answered, " She has but followed the common destiny of all, and passed beneath the tree of good and evil like the rest."*

This aphorism must have seemed inspired to the Jagunços, for it passed almost into a proverb in the Sertão during the prophet's reign. Its ferocious cynicism does not appear to have occurred to them. The phrase, with its flavour of the Scriptures, no doubt appeared to them dictated from on high. Thus did the prophet Samuel hew Agag in pieces before the Lord, regardless of all honour and all faith, and ride off on a phrase. Each day the prophet gave his counsels to the faithful, pointing out the way that they should go, and now and then performing miracles.

One day a follower wasted with fasting came to visit him, and was invited to sit down to share his frugal meal. When he departed he proclaimed, though he had eaten hardly anything, he felt as if he

* " Segiúo o destino de todas, passou por baxio da arvore do bem e do mal."

had risen from a banquet, strong and refreshed with meat. The wondrous news ran through the town and all rejoiced, both at the miracle and because it was a sign the Lord had given to their Councillor. Whether Antonio Conselheiro wished to bring the people's bodies low by fasting and thus exalt their minds, no one can say ; but it is certain that the whole population of Canudos lived, as it were, upon a pilgrimage of body and of mind. A people in this state is moved more easily to acts of heroism and of self-abnegation than those who pass an ordinary life, marrying and giving in marriage, buying and selling and setting down accounts by double entry. The greater part of the prophet's followers were simple folk, who no doubt really thought the destruction of the world was close at hand, and practised fasting and the rites of their religion in absolute good faith. Others arrived, of a far different complexion ; these he accepted without a question, holding, perhaps, that their adhesion to his cause wiped out their crimes ; or, understanding that if the aim is sure, it matters little if the hand that fires the gun be steeped in villainy. So, homicides and cattle-stealers, the broken men of the Sertão, flocked to Canudos, and were received into the fold.

Soon round him was assembled a sort of Hallelujah-band of bravos, much like the Danites who surrounded Brigham Young at Salt Lake City in the first days of Mormonism. The finest flower of all the rascaldom of the Jagunços flocked to Canudos to form his body-guard. They all held human life at a low price, for they had risked their own a hundred times in desperate enterprises. All were good horsemen, able with lazo and with lance, and all were men accustomed to the knife, for they had used it many a time at fair and pilgrimage. All carried guns of varying patterns, and used them handily, and not a rascal of them all but owed a life or two.

José Venancio, the terror of Volta Grande, who had committed half a dozen homicides, appeared one day before Antonio Conselheiro, and, kneeling in the dust, beat with his hands upon his breast, saying he was a miserable sinner and imploring to be saved. The prophet pardoned him, and took him straightway into favour, without, as it appears, even the vain formality of telling him to sin no more and to live virtuously.

Then appeared Pajehú, a ruffian who had committed innumerable crimes, but a born genius as a bush-fighter and a partisan. Tall and well made, his face was flat and negro-looking, his limbs athletic, and his whole air that of a murderer and an assassin steeped in villainy. The prophet, knowing his value as a guerilla leader, for he had proved it in a dozen skirmishes, made him his adjutant. Lolau, another scoundrel of the same kidney and a friend of Pajehú, arrived and also bent the knee before the prophet, holding his rifle in his hand.

Chiquinho and João da Motta, brothers and highwaymen, grovelled before the altar like a pair of "sacred wolves." They were named corporals of the guard of vigilantes, whose task it was to watch the entrance to the town, just at the junction of the rivers Cocorobó and Uaui where they fell into the main stream. Pedro, a bestial Cafuz,* with thirty chosen men, occupied the slopes of the little hill called Canna Brava. Estevam, a negro, whose body, all scarred over with old knife and bullet wounds, seemed to have been tattooed, guarded the Cumbaio. Joaquim Trancapes† had the care of Angico, another strategic point. "Major" Sariema, a man of better education than the rest, fearless and turbulent, had no particular charge confided to him, but led the wilder spirits in every charge during the siege until he met his death. Raymundo Bocca-Torta,‡ from Itapicurú, half comic and half tragic in his aspect, also arrived to lend his look as of a low comedian crossed with a gallows bird. The fawn-like Chico Ema, afterwards head of the scouts, with a guerilla leader of some repute called Norberto, joined the pious ranks, and fought unto the death during the last days of the Zion they had elected to defend. Quimquim de Coiqui, a man who had abjured all kinds of religion, felt his heart touched, and once again bowed his head reverently, and passed his beads between his fingers as he wept before the cross.

Antonio Fogueteiro, an ex-lay preacher, proved indefatigable in making proselytes. José Gamo, a cattle-thief, and Fabricio de Cocoboco, who seems to have had no special qualifications except his faith, were amongst the proselytes.

Foreign to the general credulity, the asute Villa Nova offered his services, and on his knees before the

* Half-breed, between Indian and negro.
† The tripper. Trancar is "to trip up."
‡ Wrymouth.

altar aped those who prayed and beat upon their breasts, although his thoughts were probably fixed on his nefarious schemes.   Old Macambora, not anxious for the fray, and known as Soft-Heart,* with his son Joaquim rode up one day and, getting off their horses, threw themselves on the ground before the prophet, and swore him fealty.   Although "soft-hearted" in the Jagunço phrase, old Macambora still was dangerous.   Famous in council, his scheming brain conceived the plans for the most part of the surprises and the ambushes that cost the Government so many soldiers, though he himself kept out of danger and never risked his life.   His son Joaquim, though but a boy in years, perished heroically.

Antonio Beato, a lean mulatto, rendered leaner still by fasting, furnished the comic element, and was, in fact, one of those semi-madmen who appear in times of difficulty and of revolt.   Half soldier and half sacristan, he bore a missal in one hand and in the other carried a blunderbuss.   Antonio Conselheiro used him as a spy upon his followers, and he transmitted to his chief all that he heard about town.   No one was safe from the half-witted yet astute mulatto, and as he passed along the street all conversations ceased till he was gone.

One man alone was innocent and pure in life and spent his time in doing good.   This was the " Curandeiro,"† Manoel Quadrado, who looked at all he saw with the most complete indifference, passing his time in gathering simples in the woods.

---

* Coração Molle.   † Hedge doctor.

José Felix, known as Taramella,* with Antonio Beato, guarded the sanctuary, and had the keys of the great trunks in which were stored the miserable robes used for processions and for ceremonies.

Lastly the governor (Chefe do Povo), João Abbade, astute and dominating, had the charge of keeping order amongst the civil population, a task that he discharged with great ability, as he understood his countrymen and their mentality. Surrounded by this bodyguard of scoundrels and fanatics, Antonio Conselheiro disposed of absolute authority over his followers. This he does not seem to have abused or used for his own benefit, but turned it all to his religious ends for disciplining life. Prayers grew and were extended daily, and litanies lasted for hours ; but the supreme and culminating moment was " the kissing of the saints."

Slowly up the church Antonio Beato advanced, with the peculiar swinging of the haunches of the mulatto, holding a crucifix. Upon the altar steps he turned towards the congregation, with the look of a fakir in ecstasy. Pressing the crucifix close to his breast, he fell down prone upon the ground, kissing it fervently.

He gave the crucifix to the nearest worshipper, who kissed and passed it on. So round the church it circulated, followed by the images of saints, which all devoutly passed from hand to hand amongst the faithful, and were devoutly kissed.

A scene of ever rising religious erethism was the result. Groans, cries, and sobs broke from the overstrained assemblage. Women fell down and writhed

* The mill-clapper—*i.e.*, chatterer.

upon the ground, exclaiming, " Jesus ! Jesus !" Children screamed and clutched their mothers' shawls. The rude Vaqueiros beat their breasts, whilst the tears trickled down their cheeks.   A thrill as of religious erotomania shook every limb, distorting every countenance into a sort of grin, half amorous, half demoniacal.   Even the leaders yielded to it.   The hideous Pajehú threw his arms round a "sister" fervently, whilst old Macamboro leered upon a maiden of fifteen with an expression like a pious satyr "cut in ebony." The others yelled, and brandishing their arms, shouted their war-cries as if they wished to take heaven by assault, carrying their prophet with them to establish him on high.

Suddenly all was stilled, as if by magic, and every eye was turned towards Antonio Conselheiro, who stood beside a table in the chancel beckoning for silence with his hand, after the manner of St. Paul upon the Areopagus.

CHAPTER VIII

In a low voice, and with his eyes fixed on the ground, he began to speak to the assembled multitude, through which a sort of ripple ran, just as it runs through a calm sea after a violent storm.

The enormous half-finished temple was packed to overflowing with a crowd mostly composed of women dressed in dirty white. Here and there men and youths were scattered, and in a clump close to the door stood the redoubtable guerilla leaders, all armed to the teeth. The temple still was open to the skies, crossed here and there by beams which were to hold up the projected roof. The atmosphere was heated like a stove. Little by little the speaker warmed up to his work, lifted his head, and broke out into invective against the republic and its work. God had forsaken all its agents. The impious ministers wished to destroy religion, and to turn everyone into mere atheists, only fit for hell. If it prevailed the reign of Antichrist was assured. At the mention of the awful name the audience broke out into cries of " Jesus, Jesus!" "Long live our good Councillor!" "Long live God!" The preacher's eyes seemed to flash fire. No one dared look him in the face. The women veiled their heads in their dingy whitish mantles, children cowered beside them, clutching at their hands; even the leather-clad Jagunços were moved, and the tears trickled down their cheeks hardened by the sun and cold. Only their leaders kept up a semblance of stoicism, but raised their arms into the air, brandishing knives and guns. The orator paused for a moment, throwing back his fell of hair. The perspiration poured down his face. Then he struck into a vein of prophecy. The reign of God was nigh. He would descend in majesty and might, confound His enemies, and destroy the impious republic; cast down the mighty from their seats; exalt the sufferers, the poor—His poor—and burn up those who had refused to come and listen to His Councillor. When the demoniac republic had disappeared, the King, Don Sebastian, should reign again for a brief space in glory, before the destruction of the world. Then, little by little, Antonio Conselheiro finished his discourse, till, at the end of it, he once more stood with his eyes upon the ground, muttering half-broken phrases, as in an ecstasy. When he had ceased, the effect upon the congregation was electric. Groans, sighs, and broken exclamations burst out, and the assemblage seemed as if a magnetic current had been applied to it, for it trilled and shivered in an orgasm of faith.

Slowly it filed out of the building and dispersed, and soon Canudos, exhausted by its faith, was silent, its people sleeping off their debauch.

Rude rhymes celebrated what they had heard in halting strophes. Some of them have been preserved, such as " Antichrist was born to govern poor Brazil, but God raised up our Councillor to save us from that ill."* " Our King, Don Sebastian, will come to visit us, and free us from the reign of the dog."† These rude effusions show the intellect and the faith of the prophet's followers. He himself could have but a vague idea of a republic, and as far as can be seen it had not troubled him in any way, whilst his revolt was entirely concerned with spiritual affairs. In reality the Sertanejos cared no more for the Emperor than for the President, or understood the principles of either government. All that they wanted was to be allowed to live their lives in their own fashion, herding their cattle, listening to sermons, singing endless hymns, and deciding personal disputes with blunderbuss or knife, after the fashion of their ancestors, the Bandeirantes,‡ who had settled up the land.

Antonio Conselheiro himself did not so much rebel against authority as against life, perhaps expecting from it more than it had to give upon the spiritual side, not understanding that a fine day, with health to enjoy it, is the most spiritual of the pleasures open to mankind. However, Antonio Conselheiro was not always in the clouds, or in the pulpit preaching to his

* " O Anti-Christo nasceu
    Paro o Brazil governar
    Mas ahi esta O Conselheiro
    Para delle nos livrar."

† " Visita nos vena fazer
    Nosso rei Don Sebastião
    Coitado daquelle pobre
    Que estiver na lei do cão."

‡ See Introduction.

followers. Like other mystics, he had an intensely practical side. He was to be observed all day superintending those whose task was to dig trenches and to construct lines of embankments along the river, behind which riflemen could lie. One thing above all others claimed his especial care. This was to build a temple worthy of the place, large enough to hold the enormous congregations that assembled in it, and to sustain the dignity that must attach to the last church built before the destruction of the world. The faithful gave their work gratuitously. Material was brought from every district of the Sertão, and piles of wood, of stone, and tiles were heaped on every side of the chief square. The builders laboured with the assiduity of ants, possessed, in addition to their instinct, of a religious fervour that drove them to their work. Since the building of the pyramids mankind could not have seen such crowds of unskilled labourers carrying beams and stones for their vast enterprise. The difference was that in Canudos all worked voluntarily, without an overseer except their Councillor himself. Early and late he was amongst his labourers, speaking to no one, but seeing everything. Nothing appears to have daunted him. The frigid mornings of the Sertão, with the thermometer well below freezing-point, found him at daylight, bareheaded, dressed in his cotton tunic, labouring at his post.

At noonday, when the fierce sun, even after frosty mornings, pours down like molten lead upon the argillaceous earth of the barren hills around Canudos, he was still upon his rounds. His workmen saw him with admiration, mixed with fear, walk like a tight-rope dancer or a somnambulist across beams passing between the walls, at a prodigious height, as little moved as when he walked upon the ground. Slowly the monstrous Babylonic edifice arose within a mass of rustic scaffolding sustained by ropes made of raw hide, or merely of lianas cut down from the trees. Shortly it dominated the whole town, towering above the humble parish church of the Fazenda, which it soon dwarfed and rendered insignificant. Built solidly in a rectangular construction, giving it the look of a medieval or of a prehistoric fortress reared by some Nimrod to reach to heaven and dominate mankind, it towered above the town. In the dead-looking land-scape, where few trees but the Mangabeira* stand the terrific and brusque alterations of the temperature and still retain their leaves, the giant temple loomed up menacing and brown. Its walls were brown, the prevailing colour of the stone of the Sertão. The outspreading sea of huts was brown and dingy-looking. Outside the boundaries and across the River Vasa-Barris the low and undulating hills looked calcined, and as barren as the mountains of the moon. Most of the workers wore the deerskin dress of the Vaqueiros, and laboured in a cloud of dust that dyed their faces even a deeper brown.

The dust hung over everything, rendering Canudos and its rising temple almost invisible within its folds, regarded from a little distance off. A traveller passing on the hills must have seen nothing but the simoon

* _Ribeirea sorbilis._

raised by the barefooted workers, pierced by the high walls of the rising temple, and by the cries of those who laboured at the task, sheltered and cut off from mankind.   The temple of the Jagunço Zion was never finished; but still it played its part in the siege that was to come.   Meanwhile, like a second Birs-Nimrod it towered above the brown, low rancheria* of the sectaries.

The Government, far away in Rio de Janeiro, was no doubt but imperfectly informed of what was going on in the Sertão.   It saw at first merely a monarchist reaction of which Antonio Conselheiro was the head.   In the chief newspapers of Rio de Janeiro articles used to appear, speaking of the Sertão as a second La Vendée, and hinting that European money was fomenting plans against " our freedom," and endeavouring "to plant once more the iron claw of the Imperial eagle in the heart of our beloved native land."   It may be that these articles were directed at conspirators in the capital itself, after the usual fashion of all Governments that never like to take the straight road when a crooked path can possibly be found.   They must have known that in the Sertão the people really did not care for any Government, and it was patent to all Brazil that the Emperor Don Pedro, a quiet, scientific man, was quite delighted to have done with politics and to retire into his laboratory.   Before resorting to the principle of force by which all Governments must ultimately

---

* " Rancheria " is the word generally applied to a collection of Indian or negro huts throughout the Americas.   We have no word in English for it, as we have no such assemblages of huts.

stand, the central authority sent up a missionary to endeavour to persuade the revolutionaries to come into the fold.

In 1895, on a May evening, there appeared upon one of the low hills that overlooked Canudos a figure of a kind hitherto not seen by the inhabitants since they had built their town. Frei João Evangelista de Monte Marciano was the emissary. Himself a Capuchin and a man of letters,* he was accompanied by two companions, the Vicar of Cumbé, who had already quarrelled with the prophet, and another Capuchin, Frei Caetano de S. Leo. All three must have been men of resolution and of courage to put their heads into the lion's den, unarmed and unsustained by any following.

Slowly they walked into the town, to the amazement of its inhabitants. Frei Monte Marciano bore a crucifix, and all the three advanced chanting a litany, a sort of " morituri te salutemus," as it were, before the sacrifice. In his own " Relatorio " Frei Monte Marciano tells us that " the chief square was packed with people crowding one upon another," that " all were armed to the teeth with guns and knives, with swords and iron-tipped cattle-goads." All this does not appear to have intimidated him or his companions in their apostolic raid.

They passed before the ancient church of the Fazenda, now turned into a chapel, and kept on upon their way through a dense multitude. They entered into a dark, winding lane in which the

---

* In his " Relatorio " he has set down the results of his mission, and given a most interesting account of Canudos.

inhabitants all came out to their doors "with an unquiet air, sinister and inquiring, that spoke of disturbed consciences and hostile intents," as the brave friar has set down in his "Relatorio." The Vicar of Cumbé had an official residence in the old village, now become a town. To this the triad bent their steps, and found it shut up, falling into decay. Round it were gathered groups of men, all armed, who glared at them without a word. Their position was not pleasant, and their disgust and apprehension were increased by the sight of eight dead bodies borne to the cemetery without the outward signs of Christian burial. Armed ruffians bore along the bodies at a trot, wrapped in their hammocks, as if, in the striking phrase used by Euclydes da Cunha in describing it, "a dead man in that city was a deserter from his martyrdom, fit to be buried like a dog."

The news of the arrival of the emissaries reached Antonio Conselheiro, at his daily task of overseeing. He took no notice of it, but went on with his work as usual, and then, entering the chapel, fell to his daily prayers. The missionaries, thus rebuffed, were forced to go to him, and turning back again through the dark, winding lane amongst a crowd ever increasing in hostility, at last they reached the church. Opening the door, they gave the usual salutation, "Praised be our Lord Jesus Christ," and to their joy Antonio Conselheiro advanced and answered them, "Let the good Lord be praised for ever," so they knew that they were safe.

Frei Monte Marciano was much impressed by the appearance of the prophet and his "air of penitence."

"His long and uncombed hair was beginning to turn grey; his face, worn with fasting, looked like that of a corpse as he advanced to meet us down the church." Antonio Conselheiro appeared to be pleased with the visit of the friars, and leaning on his pilgrim's staff, his frail and wasted body bent a little forward, he welcomed them cordially. For once he appears to have laid aside his habitual reserve. He told them how his work was getting on, offered to show them round the church, and then, going in front, acted as guide, stopping occasionally in an access of coughing, which shook him so terribly that Frei Monte Marciano feared he might expire.

The friars were astonished, for they had expected quite another kind of welcome into the lion's den. They thought their victory was half gained already, and their spirits rose, for little did they know that the frail body leaning on its staff contained an iron will. This failure to appreciate the man with whom they had to deal led them into a fatal error that they were never able to retrieve. As they walked through the church, it gradually filled with curious onlookers; for strangers in Canudos were a rare spectacle, especially friars. When they arrived at the choir, Frei Monte Marciano, turning round, addressed the multitude. Raising his voice with confidence, as if he had been preaching in his own monastery, he launched into one of those well-meaning but tactless harangues that upon like occasions have so often added fuel to the fire.

"I take this opportunity," so he said, "in the name of the Archbishop, to call upon you all to disperse and return to your homes, for this will be both for your own and for the general good." Much more he said, all quite within the bounds of common sense, and applicable enough had he been speaking to an ordinary crowd. He spoke of all the assembled people were enduring, of the bodies hurried to the grave without a prayer that he had seen during the morning, and on the danger of the gathering together of such a multitude in arms.

His courage certainly was great, but his discretion not in proportion to it, for his harangue at once stirred up his auditors to fury, and they broke into shouts of "Death to the friar! Long live our Councillor!" The imprudent friar's life hung by a thread, but Antonio Conselheiro stilled the tumult with a movement of his hand. Turning towards the friar, he said : "These people that you see in arms have all assembled only to guard me from my foes. You may remember a little time ago at Masseté the impious republic wished to slay me, and there was fighting and deaths upon both sides. In the time of the monarchy I allowed myself to be apprehended quietly, because I recognised the Government. To-day I defend myself, for I refuse to recognise the republic, or any of its works."

This explanation, quietly conveyed in a respectful tone, was not sufficient for the Capuchin. With a zeal worthy of a martyr, he began to explain the attitude of Rome towards all Governments, explaining that in France, which for the last twenty years had been a republic, the Church recognised the laws. He might have said that the Apostle Paul, as far as we know, bowed to the authority of Nero, taking apparently no heed of the proceedings in the Golden House, the slaying of the Christians, or of the burning of the town.   This, of course, might have been, as the proverb says, putting himself into a shirt of eleven yards in breadth,* for certainly none of his auditory could have heard of Nero, and not too many of St. Paul.

" Even here in Brazil," said the intrepid friar, " we all, from the Archbishop downwards, recognise the actual Government, and only you and these, your followers, refuse.   Your doctrine must be false !"   A shout broke from the Jagunços assembled in the church : " No, your reverence it is that has false doctrine ; our Councillor, the right."

A slow and sweeping gesture from the prophet stilled the tumult once again, and he said quietly, " I will not tell my followers to disarm themselves, nor yet disperse and return to their homes.   At the same time I will do nothing to disturb the holy mission of your reverence."

Word had gone round that the prophet was in danger, and the Jagunços, to the number of five thousand, hurried to the square, their bandoliers all full of cartridges and with their weapons in their hands.   Inside, the church was packed, and when the friar mounted into the pulpit towards which Antonio Conselheiro motioned him, with a courteous gesture of the hand, he gazed upon a veritable sea.   Without a text he launched into his discourse.   The congregation every now and then broke into protests at doctrines differing so widely from those their

* " Meterse en camisa de once varas."

9

Councillor was wont to preach to them. He himself, standing by the altar, now and then gravely bent his head in sign of approbation when the protests grew more vehement and loud. Frei Monte Marciano touched upon topics that he thought would commend themselves to his vast congregation ; fasting, especially, occupied a portion of the discourse. He said that fasting was enjoined, not to destroy the bodies of mankind, but to restrain their passions, and that a man might eat sufficient meat to keep him in good health and yet commit no sin. In fact, he preached a sermon of the kind known to Scotch theologians as Erastian, a mere cold morality, very unsatisfying to the soul. When he explained his theory of fasting the Jagunços broke into a laugh, and one exclaimed, " That is not fasting, but mere gormandising." His sermon finished in Homeric laughter and in jeers; but the friar still persisted for four days, in spite of being branded a Freemason and a Protestant-Republican.

He also was accused of being a mere emissary of the Government, sent to distract the attention of people till the troops should arrive. The last time that the imprudent friar addressed his unwilling hearers was on homicide. No theme could have been less acceptable to men accustomed from their youth to violence. Their attitude became so hostile that there was nothing left him, if he aspired to save his life, but to retreat, and that as speedily as he was ready for the road. His undaunted courage and his zeal were wasted—that is, if the exercise of zeal and courage are ever really wasted—or exercised in vain. In the material field, on which alone the vulgar estimate that

most vulgar of results, success, he achieved little, failing where men as zealous and undaunted as himself
have often failed before.   Fifty-five couples who had
been living in open scandal and in sin, to their own
satisfaction, he joined in wedlock, blotting out the sin,
but not the scandal, as that had passed into the region
of things done, beyond the power of mitigation or
recall.

He and his followers heard several hundred general
confessions, which must have been extended to some
length, for there was plenty to confess.

Not much achieved, for all the danger he had run ;
but then the field was stony, as are the pastures in the
uplands of Castile, outside of Avila.

When they came to a little hill, Frei Monte
Marciano and his two companions halted ; then, taking
off their sandals, they shook the dust from them
against Canudos, and after having launched the curse
of Rome against the place and its inhabitants, they
bent their steps towards a more favourable field.

CHAPTER IX

THE mission having failed ignominiously, there was no resource left to the Government but an appeal to arms. At that time the central authority of the new republic was not thoroughly established, and throughout the country various revolutionary movements were going on to combat it.

The city of Lençoes was besieged by brigands. Towards the territory in which are situated the diamond mines all was confusion, and in Rio Grande do Sul military operations were taking place. Situated as it was, the Government found it impossible to send an expedition against Canudos for a considerable time. This gave Antonio Conselheiro time to consolidate his position and to receive great reinforcements from the surrounding districts of the Sertão.

For at least two hundred years the territory immediately to the west of the district of Canudos had been a prey to social turmoil; for it was there, attracted by the gold and diamond mines, that the most turbulent elements of the population of Brazil found a congenial home. All those who did not like a settled life of work came to the territory, ostensibly to seek for mines, but in reality to live by rapine and by crime.

There, the Jagunço was preceded by the Garimpeiro, a predatory rascal who lived by stealing cattle and by pillaging outlying farms. He, in his turn, was helped by the Capungueiro or outcast from the towns, who found the life congenial to him and became as savage as the Indians. The territory between the rivers Vasa-Barris and São Francisco stretching north and south, and from Canudos westward to the Rio das Egoas,* had thus become a veritable no-man's-land. In 1804 Caetano Pinto de Miranda Montenegro, a traveller who has left much curious information as to his wanderings at that epoch, writes of it : " Coming from Cuyabá to the Recife,† a journey of six hundred and seventy leagues . . . I formed the opinion that in no portion of the dominions of the King of Portugal‡ is human life less safe "—this though he had traversed leagues of virgin forest exposed to the attacks of the wild Indians, and though Cuyabá itself was a remote and frontier village, situated at the extreme limits of the empire, and took three months to reach. A more modern writer, Colonel Durval, puts it on record that " anyone who has to travel through the territory must lay in a great stock of all provisions and be well armed, for at that price alone will he achieve his journey in security." The whole face of the country was undulating, broken by hills, cut here and there with islands of forest that jutted out into the elevated plains called Taboleiros,

* River of the Mares, probably so called from the herds of wild horses that frequented its banks in old times.

† Recife = Pernambuco, so called from the great reef (recife) that forms the harbour.

‡ Brazil was then a Portuguese colony.

which were studded with cactus, dwarf palms, and scrubby bush. In the plains the grass was good, and capable of sustaining considerable herds of cattle—had there been security for property and life. As it was, these were but scantily grazed upon, and that to a considerable disadvantage, as owing to the sparse populations, jaguars from the surrounding forest did great damage to the herds.

Houses were rare and travellers infrequent, and on the plains or in the forest trails strangers on meeting manœuvred, as it were, for the weather gauge. They shouted out their salutations from afar, each with his hand close to his gun, holding his horse upon the bit, ready to pull his head up to receive a shot aimed at the rider, or dash aside should the stranger endeavour to close in. Men on a journey in the district kept their eyes fixed on the horizon to discover dust rising, or the smoke issuing from a burning house, or on the ground to mark the trail of any passer-by upon the road. Strangers were enemies, and dust, or smoke, fresh broken branches on a bush, or grass just trodden down, the flight of birds, or the uneasy movement of the cattle on the plains, warned travellers to be upon the watch.

The scattered towns were fallen into decay, although recovering about the time when the prophet founded Canudos ; but they were many leagues apart from one another. The mining town of Januaria, in 1879, was conquered by a band of Jagunços from a place called Carinhanha, who sacked it and returned laden with the spoil. Pilão Arcado, once flourishing, but now (1918) deserted, suffered the same fate, after a great raid that took place in 1856. Xigue-Xigue, Machubas, Monte Alegre, and innumerable fazendas were pillaged and left desolate at a comparatively recent date. One town alone had escaped amongst the general ruin of the rest. This was Bom Jesus da Lapa, the Mecca of the Sertanejos, held inviolate. Its fine position on a hill made it remarkable. Near it existed a strange cave, whose stalactites and stalagmites gave it the appearance of a church not made with hands, but built by Nature for the worship of the great forces that had created it. Its long and tortuous passages were full of bones of ancient animals, and that no circumstance should be wanting to contribute to its sanctity a curious legend rose.

There, it was said, once lived a penitent, a man who, having soiled his soul with deeds of violence, had retired into the desert to pass his life in prayer for the remission of his sins. A jaguar, attracted by his sanctity, kept him supplied with food. Thus sanctified by Nature and religion, the place became a goal of pilgrimages for the inhabitants of all the Sertoès, from distant Piauhy and from Sergipe, down to the borders of Goyáz.

Upon the walls of the chapel of the sanctuary were hung numerous votive offerings as is customary in sites of pilgrimages, where legs and arms and fingers, moulded in wax, attest the cures vouchsafed, or ships are hung by pious mariners who have escaped a storm.

In the chapel of the Bom Jesus da Lapa were hung up guns and knives. Bandits who entered fully armed were awestruck, and, bursting into tears, felt their souls touched with ecstasy. They thought upon the crimes they had committed, most likely with the very arms they carried in their hands. A loathing seized them, as it so often seizes drunkards after a debauch. At once they made a resolution to sin no more, and to remove temptation from their hands hung up their instruments of crime before the Infant Jesus and fell upon the ground. No doubt they felt relieved when they had thus poured out their souls and given up their arms into the keeping of the sacred Child, who smiled upon them from the walls. Their repentance was sincere, as all repentances are quite sincere, so far as they are movements of the grace interior. As they passed out into the sun they must have felt new men, chastened and lightened of the burden of their crimes. Perhaps they felt pangs of regret at leaving the blunderbuss upon whose stock was cut in crosses the number of the lives they owed, just as men always feel regret to leave behind them an old comrade or a piece of well-remembered furniture.

However, life in the Sertão had its own complications and its exigencies. The chiefest is the means of self-defence, for there, above all places in the world, man is the wolf of man. Most likely in a day or two, finding themselves, as they would say, " sem sombra,"* when deprived of arms, they took the road to the first town and purchased better and more modern weapons to carry on the fight. Of the three forces that beset mankind—the world, the devil, and the flesh—the world is the most potent enemy, for it

* Literally, "without shade," the sun being the enemy in lands of sun.

includes the other two, and its attacks are far more subtle and far harder to resist.

As no society, even in a robbers' cave, can live without some ordinances, or at the least some bye-laws for its own protection, a curious custom had arisen in this most turbulent of all the districts of Brazil. It was well recognised that farms and cattle, even towns, were liable to be attacked, pillaged, or carried off ; but by a curious distinction, with rare exceptions, individual property was safe. Thus a man, even without arms, could traverse the wild district on the banks of the Rio das Egoas on his journey to the coast, although his saddle-bags were full of gold-dust or diamonds from the mines. In the same way a stranger who had no part in any of the factions that abounded and made desolate the land was equally secure. Sometimes a pedlar leading a pack mule would at the crossing of some stream, or on a lonely track meandering through the impenetrable woods, find himself suddenly confronted with a band of bandits all armed to the teeth. The chief would usually approach him, as he sat trembling on his mule, and pass the time of day. Then he would ask him for a handful of cigars, throw his leg over his horse's neck, and sitting sideways, light one of them with his flint and steel, then, after handing out the rest amongst his followers, turn to the pedlar and bid him " go with God," and the whole troop would disappear into the woods.

As the news of the building of Canudos slowly percolated through this wild district, bringing with it the tidings that not only would the man who joined

Antonio Conselheiro be in safety from all pursuit of the authorities, but would be preserved from the destruction of mankind so soon to come about, than hundreds of its wild inhabitants flocked to the prophet's side. Canudos formed the point of junction for all the roving bands of bandits, of cattle thieves and broken men, who for years past had infested all the territory between the River São Francisco and the Rio das Egoas—in fact, from Piauhy down to the province of Goyáz.

These men, though robbers, and in most cases murderers, were deeply tinged with religion (or superstition), and the fame of Antonio Conselheiro's preaching, joined to his opposition to the Government, drew them like iron towards a magnet, and of course greatly increased his power. After the failure of the mission of the friars, the Government seems to have determined on a policy of inactivity, hoping perhaps that when the novelty wore off the movement soon would disappear. If they had any such design, it shows their absolute misconception of the character of the inhabitants of the Sertão. Slow to decide, and indolent, as was their usual attitude, no people in the world was more determined, or less daunted by ill-fortune when once the die was cast. Unlike their Gaucho cousins on the plains of Rio Grande or in the Argentine—men ready to revolt or follow any leader, turbulent, but yet inconstant, soon discouraged, and ready to disband their forces and return to their homes—the Sertanejos were of adamant. Misfortune only made them more determined, and they were always most to be feared after a check or a defeat. On such occasions a surprise attack was always to be expected from them. The rugged nature of their country, with its hard climate and its pathless wilds, was greatly in their favour for all such enterprises and for ambushes. Their upbringing, always at war with Nature, their tinge of Indian blood, and their religious fervour, made them an enemy never to be despised by those who knew them best. This was the error of the Government, who held them cheaply for their want of discipline.

In 1896 the storm, which had so long been brewing, burst out with violence.

CHAPTER X

JUST as in greater States wars frequently break out from insufficient or from futile causes, so in the small community of the Sertão hostilities between the prophet's followers and the republic were brought about by a small matter, not worth the sacrifice of life. No doubt the real cause lay deeper, as is usually the case in wars waged by more formidable powers.

Antonio Conselheiro had contracted in the town of Joazeiro, not far off from the River São Francisco, for a quantity of wood. The contract happened to have been made with two town councillors or magistrates. When the time expired some difficulty arose as to the delivery. This was accentuated by the fact that the contractor, a year or two before, happening to be at that time a judge in Bom Conselho, had, after a dispute, been chased out of the town by the prophet's followers and put in danger of his life. Whether he wished to avenge the insult or really was unable to implement his bargain, only himself could tell. At any rate, the wood was not forthcoming at the appointed time, and after several unavailing protests Antonio Conselheiro prepared to attack the town with a strong party of his followers.

Times had changed since he bowed his head

beneath the insults of the world. Now he stood forth
a leader and a redresser of abuses, little disposed to
sit down patiently under injustices. In 1897 the
Governor of the State of Bahia wrote to the President
of the Republic in the following terms :

" I have received," he said, " from Dr. Arlindo
Leoni, Judge of the district of Joazeiro, an urgent
telegram telling me that in a day or two his town will
be attacked by Antonio Conselheiro and his followers,
and asking me for help to stay the panic and the
exodus already taking place. I answered him that I
could not send troops upon a simple rumour, and recom-
mended him to guard the approaches to the town, and
if he saw the rebels really advance, send me a telegram ;
then I would succour him with a military force. . . .
I ordered the General in command of the district to
send a hundred men to Joazeiro as soon as he received
a message from the Judge that they were necessary to
repel attack. The Judge informed me that Antonio
Conselheiro's forces were about two days' journey from
the town, so I have now despatched the soldiers under
Lieutenant Pires Feireira to join the forces of the
town."

From such a little matter, the mere refusal to
implement a contract, great events were destined to
ensue. For the past quarter of a century, in fact since
1874, Antonio Conselheiro had been known in the
Sertão. Little by little his fame had increased in all
the district, and the traces of his passage were manifest
in every village and each town. Here was a chapel,
there a church, and farther on a cemetery, raised from
a state of ruin and decay, rebuilt, or re-enclosed

entirely by his efforts and by the labour of his followers.

Upon the whole, in the material sense, his influence had made for good; for though he did but little towards establishing a reasonable line of conduct, he was a rallying-point for people who felt themselves deserted absolutely by all the powers that be. His influence was great because of the success of his last exploits. In 1893, at Masseté, he had gained a victory in the field, and later on a moral victory, when the troops sent against him had returned without a blow struck or a shot fired, simply before the terror of his name.

The apostolic mission of the Capuchin had been a failure, and from all sides recruits continued to arrive. Frei Monte Marciano has left on record, in his "Relatorio," that the armed forces in Canudos at the time of his apostolic visit numbered about "a thousand men, all armed and vigorous." The town itself was situated in a position naturally strong, and above all Antonio Conselheiro had the advantage of public sympathy, for the whole district deemed him a saviour.

Against this town, situated in such a good position for defence and so well garrisoned and amply provisioned, the Government sent only a hundred soldiers of the line. These were to join the half-armed, semi-disciplined and scanty militia of the town of Joazeiro —an inconsiderable force. This was to court defeat. So little did the Government understand the seriousness of the campaign in front of them, that, in November, 1896, General Federico Solon, in command of the district, wrote to the General saying he had received orders to march against Canudos with a force of about one hundred soldiers, and judged them amply numerous enough for what he had to do. On the 7th of November they arrived in Joazeiro, to the astonishment of the inhabitants, who knew the strength of the Jagunços advancing to attack. At once there was a general exodus, families fleeing with their children and such portion of their household goods as could be carried upon carts. As always happens in such circumstances, the town was full of people well disposed towards the sectaries. All these were over-joyed, and secretly sent out messengers to the Jagunços, telling them the small number of the troops.

The difficulties of transport and of provisions were enormous, for beyond Joazeiro no food was to be obtained ; pasture and grass were scarce, roads non-existent, and the track led through deep defiles, bushy and strewn with rocks. The troops left Joazeiro on the night of the 12th, so as to avoid a start on the 13th, deemed an unlucky day.

Two hundred kilometres separated Joazeiro from the prophet's stronghold. Summer* was just begin-ing. The nights were icy, whilst the noonday sun poured down like fire, making the change of tempera-ture at sunset more difficult to bear. The wells were few and far between, and the two guides hired at Joazeiro not over trustworthy. Moreover, most of the troops were men of colour from the hot regions of the coast, unused to cold and unaccustomed to long marches amongst hills. None of them were broken to frontier warfare, and all were quite at sea in wars of ambushes, surprises, and of night alarms. The

* In the southern hemisphere.

season was unusually dry and hot, and the scant
herbage had almost disappeared. The trees began to
shed their leaves under the scorching heat, and looked
like skeletons. At the rare springs and pools the
cattle crowding to slake their thirst had trampled them
into a slough of mud. In the Sertão in summer few
people travel after ten o'clock, in the fierce heat that
turns the sandy trails into a sea of fire. Those who
are forced to do so travel on horseback or on mules.
The unlucky soldiers had to march on foot, wrapped
in a cloud of dust. The country in itself was poor,
the very scrub falling into the category of what is
known as Caatanduva*—that is, the " weak bush."
The expedition had to cross a country wild and
uncultivated, almost unknown to most Brazilians ; a
land of thirst in which all human habitations of
necessity are rare, and even these the soldiers found
deserted—an evil omen for an invading force in any
country. The first day they were forced to camp
upon the open plains only two leagues from Joazeiro,
and passed the night short of provisions and shivering
with cold.

Next day a stage of forty kilometres faced them.
Water was only to be found at a little lake called
" A lagoa do Boi,"† where still a little water lingered
in the bottom of the pool. They reached it almost
exhausted, though without attack from the Jagunços,
and slept upon the ground, far too fatigued to put up
tents or do more than light a fire or two. For the

* From Caa, " bushwood," and Ahiva, " weak or bad," in
Guarani or Tupi.
† The bullocks' water-hole or pool.

next few days they passed a veritable *via crucis,*
finding the villages deserted, and seeing nothing but a
few goats amongst the rocks, as shy as deer, and, now
and then, some cattle which had run half wild and
galloped off at their approach.   The mirage mocked
them, spreading illusory lakes a mile in front, and
then when they had struggled on, hoping to slake their
thirst, vanishing altogether, or moving farther off

At last, on the 19th, they reached Uauá, a miserable
village, with two straggling streets that ran into a
square, sandy and desolate, set round with cabins and
with huts.   A store or two, flat-roofed and stuccoed,
with iron-grated windows, and several hitching posts
before the door, a church in bad repair, and a series of
corrals, to which on fair days Vaqueiros drove their
cattle or their mules, were the chief feature of the
wretched little place.   The fairs held upon feast-days
were the occasions when the town put on an air of
animation, that it put off again the instant that the
fair was over, and fell back into sleep.

Throughout Brazil and in most parts of South
America the siesta wraps the world in sleep during
the hotter hours, a death-like silence steals upon the
world, and nothing but the buzzing of the flies is
heard, or the occasional stamping of a horse tied up
beneath a tree.   The flag upon the " Comandancia "
flaps lazily against the staff, like the leach of a sail
flaps in a calm, or hangs down limp like a dead vul-
ture set up to scare the parrots from a cornfield.   So
deeply are its votaries given over to their slumbers,
that a man may ride into a store through the broad
doorway, stooping a little as he passes under it, and

rap with his whip's handle on the counter; then, finding no response, wheel round his horse and ride him out again, leaving the owner of the store unaware of his visit, and still sleeping like the dead. The sleepers in the little town of Uauá were awakened by the strains of a bugle sounding in the square. The unusual sound of martial music prevailed over the habit of a lifetime, and they appeared to welcome to their town the force the Government had sent. Great was their astonishment to see halted upon the plaza the miserable, thirst-stricken, and forlorn-looking little band of soldiers that had just struggled in and thrown themselves upon the ground in weariness. The men were dusty, footsore, and tired out. Their ranks were badly dressed, and most of them carried their jackets hanging from their guns. Their officers were mounted upon mules or pack-ponies that they had bought or commandeered in Joazeiro, and the whole aspect of the little force was melancholy and dispiriting.

After a rest they set up bivouacs—for tents were non-existent as they had no pack animals to carry them. Cutting down palm-leaves, they built up little shelters against the scorching sun, and stationed sentinels at the four corners of the square in order to command the roads. Then they made coffee and ate a miserable meal, having no energy to cook after their sufferings. By all the rules of military strategy and of common-sense, they ought to have pushed on towards Canudos an hour or two before the sun was up, to avoid the heat, and to endeavour to surprise the prophet's stronghold, for in a prompt surprise lay their scant chances of success. This, the commander found impossible owing to the condition of his men and the fact that the road before them ran through a desert, in which the man who wandered from the track was doomed to death by hunger or by thirst. The guides from Joazeiro were uncertain of the track, or said they were, most likely sympathising secretly with Antonio Conselheiro, and willing to lose time.

The 20th passed in rest and in the search for information, both on the situation and the road. At nightfall the commander, going on his rounds, found the whole town deserted, for the inhabitants had silently withdrawn, either because they feared to be exposed to the attack which they looked on as certain, or on an order from the prophet sent to them secretly. This fact should have alarmed the commander of the troops had he but taken in the danger of his situation and the impossibility of receiving reinforcements at such a distance from his base. He took no heed of the occurrence, and the troops lay down beneath their bivouacs, sleeping as tranquilly as if Antonio Conselheiro and his men were all a thousand miles away from them. An hour or two before the sun rose, the favourite moment for attack on every frontier, the advance guard of the Jagunços appeared. Formed in procession, carrying banners of the saints and singing hymns, their army seemed a band of pilgrims mounting a Calvary. All were armed in some fashion or other, with guns and swords, cattle-goads, axes, scythes set upright upon poles, or some rude weapon or another which they found ready to their hands.

All carried knives, and many bore old-fashioned

flint-lock pistols and bell-mouthed blunderbusses. Some, in default of other arms, had clubs, and some rough slings, which they used commonly for herding cattle on the plains. A motley crew, but all inspired with faith in their great Councillor, who had assured them of the victory over the soldiers of the " Dog."* Some told their beads as they advanced, and some prayed loudly, brandishing their arms. Though they advanced quite openly and singing as they marched to the number of about three thousand, as an eye-witness says, they met with no resistance till they arrived upon the outskirts of the town.

Fearing an ambush, Pajehú, who was in chief command, halted his followers and stayed their psalmody, and then sent out some scouts. These penetrated to the sentinels placed at the four cross roads, and found them sleeping at their posts, and all the town asleep. As they returned with the astounding news towards the main body, they encountered three advanced guards, who, springing to their feet, fired off their carbines and retreated to the town. Roused from his slumbers, dressed in his shirt and drawers, as he had risen from his bed, the colonel in command hurried down to the plaza with a bugler by his side, who sounded the alarm.

Soldiers came scurrying from their bivouacs, and from the houses of the town, where they were sleeping to shelter from the cold, dressing and loading as they ran. Scant time they had to form their ranks, though an old sergeant died bravely at

* The " Dog " typified the republic. All its laws they called " the law of the dog "—" A lei do Cão."

his post trying to stem the tide. With yells and cries of " Bom Jesus !" and " Viva Conselheiro !" the Jagunços fell upon them. The line was never formed, and in an instant in the semi-darkness all was confusion, and the troops struggled for their lives. The instinct of self-preservation, or the remains of discipline, made them stand together and retreat towards the houses, where they re-formed and fired upon the sectaries from windows and from doors.

This was the means of the salvation of a good many of the troops, for the Jagunços, grouped in masses on the square, replied but feebly to their fire. Huddled together like a flock of sheep, exposed to fire from modern rifles, and only able to reply with blunderbusses and old-fashioned guns, the followers of the prophet soon suffered a considerable loss. Decimated, without being able to reply, the Jagunço leaders saw their only chance was in a general attack upon the houses where the soldiers were entrenched. Grouped round their sacred banner they came on, shouting their war-cries mixed with pious adjurations, though every volley stretched dozens of them on the ground. Brandishing their goads and knives, they reached the houses where the colonel, still in his shirt and drawers, stood giving out cartridges to his fast falling men, under a heavy fire.

A sub-lieutenant, standing half naked on the bed from which he had been roused by the attack, stood bravely firing through the window, until a bullet stretched him lifeless on the bed in which so lately he had slept. It seemed as if the houses must be carried and the troops overwhelmed in the impetuous rush of the Jagunços, who came on careless of their lives, disdaining even to take cover in the fury of their charge. The rush just failed, and slowly, vociferating imprecations, the sectaries fell back, and, as by magic, all disappeared into the woods.

As they were disappearing the sun rose, as he rises in the tropics, without an interval of twilight, and in the morning light the town looked tragical. Dead bodies lay about in front of every doorstep, and blood had soaked the balconies and window frames. Three or four houses had been set on fire, and in the lurid light cast by their flames upon the scene, the wounded tried to drag themselves to shelter, whilst the exhausted soldiers, too tired to aid them, throwing themselves down half lifeless on the ground, slept as men sleep after a night of struggle for their lives.

About two hundred of the sectaries were killed or dangerously wounded, and all the latter the soldiers conscientiously put out of their suffering when they awoke from sleep. The troops had ten men killed, amongst them the brave sub-lieutenant slain upon his bed, a sergeant and the two guides that they had hired in Joazeiro. The doctor of the expedition had gone mad during the combat, either from terror or from the hardships he had undergone upon the march. Thus he was useless to the sixteen wounded, whose wounds were dressed in the best fashion they were able by their own comrades, who tore their shirts up to make bandages.

The Government had gained a Pyrrhic victory. The colonel still had sixty soldiers, unwounded but much discouraged, for, for the first time, they could appreciate the courage of the enemy and understand what difficulties lay before them if they pursued their task. Placed as he was, cumbered with wounded men tor whom he had no transport, both his guides killed, and totally without the means of getting any reinforcements, one course alone was open to the commander of the troops. At all events, he had to evacuate the place before the darkness should expose him to a fresh attack on his exhausted men. Their comrades buried hurriedly in the cemetery, the troops at once set out upon the march under the torrid sun. Most luckily for them, the Jagunços, after the check they had received, did not appear again, for had they done so not a single man would have remained alive. Four days of agony were passed upon the trail to Joazeiro, which they reached more like a mob of fugitives than like a band of soldiers who had stood bravely to their arms against superior force. The water-holes had nearly all dried up, and by the second day provisions were exhausted, and the unlucky men struggled along supporting one another, falling down but to die.

When they arrived at Joazeiro and staggered into the town, the population looked on them with amazement, so great a change had come upon them all in the disastrous campaign. Dusty and ragged, half-starved and wounded, tortured by thirst, and footsore with the road, they scarce had spirit to relate all that had happened to them. The very sight of them caused such a panic in the town that the men fit to bear arms ran armed into the square, thinking that the Jagunços might be expected to attack the town at any minute, as they supposed that they were following up the trail. Trains with their engine fires lighted and a full head of steam stood waiting in the station, ready to take the inhabitants away at the first symptom of alarm.

Nothing occurred, as the Jagunços had no idea of following up their Pyrrhic conquerors, for they knew well enough they had inflicted a reverse upon the Government.

CHAPTER XI

Rumour, ever an active agent in countries like Brazil, soon magnified the situation far beyond due bounds. The most absurd report of the strength of the forces that Antonio Conselheiro had at his disposal soon began to be believed. It was asserted that he was well supplied with arms, and with artillery, by the Monarchists. In point of fact the party favourable to a restitution of the Imperial power was negligible. No arms, except a few dozen modern rifles which had been smuggled in, had reached Canudos, and artillery there was none. Upon the other hand, the withdrawal of the Government forces had brought in hundreds of recruits, though it is most improbable that at the most the prophet ever disposed of more than five thousand fighting men, and even these were quite inadequately armed.

Still, it behoved the Government to make " an act of presence "* by fitting out an expedition large enough to ensure success. Therefore they got together a formidable force—that is, formidable for such a purpose—and one that ought to have been able to reduce the sectaries had it been rightly used.

The federal Governor wrote to the Capital demand-

* " Um acto de presença."

ing an armed force of about six hundred soldiers, with two Krupp field-guns and four Nordenfeldts. This imposing force would have seemed ridiculous for the reduction of an open village, defended but by men armed with antique weapons, had it not been for the difficulties of the road and the peculiar nature of the warfare which the last expedition had disclosed.

The whole military force was placed under the direction of Colonel Pedro Nunes Tamarindo, a man experienced in warfare, but not in the particular kind of fighting that he was called upon to meet. In the first encounter at Uauá, the Jagunços had allowed themselves to be engaged precisely in the circumstances that were unfavourable to them and advantageous to the troops. Massed in the plaza of the town, they fell in heaps when exposed to modern rifle fire. The example was a warning to them, and they never fell into the same mistake during the warfare that ensued. It is probable that in the attack on Uauá, blinded by fanaticism, and relying on superior numbers, they thought to carry everything in the first rush. They were deceived, and henceforth took full advantage of their knowledge of the Sertão, their great mobility, and of the difficult nature of the country through which the enemy was bound to pass. Few countries in the world are naturally easier to defend. The thick, impenetrable bush that juts out in islands and peninsulas into the plains, the hills covered with boulders, the tracks that wind about knee-deep in sand or mud according to the season; the want of water in the summer and the floods in winter, and above all the scarcity of provisions, render a campaign in the Sertão a formidable undertaking even to seasoned troops.

The plan of Colonel Tamarindo was to attack by means of two converging columns, and so to break the resistance of the sectaries before he had arrived at his objective, hoping that they would fall into the trap. In reality, no plan could possibly have been less likely of success in such a country and with such enemies. The governmental forces entered the town of Monte Santo on the 27th of December, 1896. This town, the birthplace of the missionary friar Appollonio de Todi,* was situated on the slope of a hill, from which all the surrounding country could be seen. It lies in the extreme north of the province of Bahia, close to the frontiers of the States of Piauhy, of Alagoas and Sergipé, not far from the River Vasa-Barris, a considerable stream. It was there that Frei Appollonio de Todi had reared his temple and made his Calvary, which, paved with pieces of the whitest quartz imaginable, winds its way up the hill. Monte Santo, situated as it was, not more than thirty kilometres from the railhead at Queimadas, formed the base of attack for all the expeditions which the Government found itself forced to send. The town had never seen so great a force, or one so well equipped with tents and military stores and with artillery. At the review the colonel held the first day after he arrived, he mustered five hundred and forty-three men of the rank-and-file, with fourteen officers and three doctors. To these were added a small artillery division with the two Krupp cannons

* See Introduction.

and the four Nordenfeldt quick-firing guns. Besides all
these there were about two hundred police. Nothing
had ever been seen before on such a scale in the
quiet town to which so many pilgrims used to resort
in times of peace. All the day long the inhabitants
were in the streets or straying close to the encampment, gazing admiringly at the new uniforms and
brilliant rifles of the soldiers, and looking with amazement at the artillery. The Vaqueiros, who had come
in from the country, tied their campeao* under a tree
and passed the day in staring at the troops. Some,
genuinely alarmed at the awful-looking guns, mounted
their horses and returned to the shelter of the Caatingas ; others, who had been sent as spies, galloped off
towards Canudos to tell what they had seen. No one
took any notice of them in the general festivities that
were taking place. So, whilst the people of the town
and all the officers of the expedition thought that
victory was secure, and a mere military procession
with a show of force would settle the whole thing,
Antonio Conselheiro was informed of the last detail
of their strength, and laid his plans to compass their
defeat. All were not thus deceived, and many of the
country people, wrapped in their ponchos, as they
lounged about the street, looked on the troops ironi-
cally, foreseeing that the festivities would end in tears,
for as they said, " They are delivered like dumb oxen
into the hands of our good Councillor."

The town authorities gave a banquet to the officers.
At this festivity the discourses, packed with allusions

---

* Literally " the Champion "—*i.e.*, the best horse. The Gauchos
use the phrase " El Credito," in the same way, for their best horse.

to " our Brazilian mothers," our " great and glorious
land," and freedom, themes which with little variation
re-occur in every speech in South America, brought
forth the usual cheers.   Our Country, Glory, and
Eternal Liberty, a goddess accountable for millions of
ineptitudes in politics and in orations, were duly
toasted.   All agreed that in a week or two, or at the
most a month, the expedition would return " bearing
the laurel with their arms."   It was the general
conviction that victory was assured, and all looked
forward to the time " when the barbarity which has
been the scandal of our native land shall disappear
and be succeeded by a reign of progress and of peace."
All this, of course, as is the case in all such speeches
and on such occasions, was to be brought about by
blood, for blood is the baptismal water by which
peace is ensured.   As peril often raises the spirits of
an army, so does the certainty of victory serve to de-
press the energy of troops, making them over-confident,
and apt to fall into a panic if anything goes wrong.
This was the case in Monte Santo, where the expedition remained for fifteen days, banqueting, speechify-
ing, and losing time.   With such an enemy as they
had to face, success depended upon speed.   Had they
marched on without delay, they might have found
Canudos unprepared, ready to fall into their hands.
As it was, the prophet had had ample time to elabo-
rate the plans for his defence.   Part of the munitions
had been left at the railhead at Queimadas, and these
had not arrived during the fifteen days that had been
spent at Monte Santo in banqueting and idleness.   As
often happens in the like circumstances after a loss

of time, there comes a fit of energy and a desire to embark at once upon the enterprise. This happened now, and Colonel Tamarindo, having left half of his munitions, determined to halve those he had with him at Monte Santo and start at once upon the track. This he did, not being able to find sufficient transport and knowing that his success depended on his speed. The resolution was fatal, and his brigade marched out to certain ruin and defeat.

Had he but followed his first plan or an advance in double columns, one marching at a little distance from the other, all might have been well. This plan would have allowed him to make use of his artillery upon a double flank, and then converge upon Canudos, as the objective of his march. Colonel Tamarindo, on the contrary, started from Monte Santo on the 13th of January (1897) in a single column, and marched in close-formed ranks. In the deep sand the marching columns suffered horribly from dust, and the men soon commenced to flag, after their period of inaction in the town. Water was scarce, and hardly to be met with, and when they were attacked their close formation made them an easy target to the hidden enemy. The road from Monte Santo to Canudos—if road it can be called, being in reality but a mere cattle track—runs through the Curiaca valley, passing at first through cultivated lands. Then it turns to the east by the slopes of Acaru and becomes stonier. From there it crosses several ridges of foothills, passing through winding bush paths, and then comes out into the open at a place called Lagem de Dentro, a sort of plateau of about nine hundred feet in height.

Here they encamped, after two days of painful marching in the sand. The two Krupp guns had terribly
delayed their progress, for the roads were so bad that
sappers had to go in front to prepare a path for them.
This took away the mobility of the column, and on
mobility depended its success. Had it been able to
arrive before Canudos in a reasonable time, and open
fire at once with its artillery well supplied with
ammunition, the campaign might have been over in a
week. As it turned out, the stars fought for the
prophet, for the commander of the forces of the
Government fell into innumerable mistakes. From
Lagem de Dentro the road runs through a deep
and narrow pass to the next halting-place, called
Ipureiras. The marches were determined, as they are
in Africa, by the distance of the water-holes. After a
long day they camped at Ipureiras, a miserable place,
with only a small water-hole, and dominated on every
side by hills. Luckily for them, the night passed
without attack. Next day they arrived at Penedo,
half-way to Canudos, and their spirits once again
began to rise. From this point, the road became even
more difficult. Cattle tracks crossed it repeatedly,
making it extremely hard to keep on the right path.
All day they weltered in the sand, without a drop of
water or a particle of shade against the sun, making
but scarce two leagues, and reaching a deserted farm,
called Mulunga, as night began to fall. Fires just extinguished, but still smouldering, told of encampments
of the enemy, and in the distance clouds of dust were
rising on the horizon far away, raised by the cattle as
they were driven in towards the town. Everything

spoke of the proximity of the enemy.   The soldiers
slept upon their arms.   During the night vague
shadows came and went near the encampment, and
once or twice the alarm was sounded, so that by
morning they were glad to leave the place.   Three
days of steady marching still intervened between them
and Canudos ; but, by this time, the condition of the
troops had become perilous.   Provisions had run low,
and, at Mulunga, they were obliged to kill their last
two bullocks, whose flesh furnished a mere mouthful
when shared amongst five or six hundred men.
Disaster stared them in the face, and, in their difficulty,
Colonel Tamarindo, being ashamed to retreat before a
shot was fired, came to the almost desperate resolution
of pushing on, hoping to take Canudos with a rush,
and then secure provisions for his men.   They started
before daylight, and the first rays of light disclosed
the fact that the men with the pack-mules, hired in
Monte Santo, had all deserted and gone back.   One
guide remained, a man called Domingos Jesuino, and
he proved loyal to them.   By devious paths he led the
column to a place called Rancho das Pedras, where
they bivouacked, being too exhausted to erect their
tents, or to do anything but sleep.

Only two leagues now separated them from Canudos, and all night long they saw the camp fires of the
Jagunços, twinkling like stars on every side of them.
Still there was no attack.   At daybreak, hungry and
footsore, they broke camp, and with their artillery
dragged along by ropes, began to move towards the
town.   In front of them rose Mount Cambaio, like
an enchanted city, its rocks worn by the weather into

pinnacles and towers.   It seemed to bar the road, but
their guide led them by a path close to the foot of it.
They passed it shuddering, waiting for the attack, so
long delayed that it had made the soldiers panicky.
Beyond Cambaio the road runs straight without a
turn, between high cliffs.   Far in the distance, like a
landscape seen at the wrong end of a telescope,
appeared Canudos, brown and menacing.

Though the road seemed quite level, there were
depressions in it, invisible till they approached them,
and in one of these, as they toiled wearily along, their
fingers on the triggers of their guns, the long expected,
long delayed attack was launched on them.   Upon the
rocks on each side of the road, as if by magic, the
Jagunços suddenly appeared.   Rifle-fire crackled to
the accompaniment of yells of " Bom Jesus !" and
" Viva Conselheiro !"   Homeric taunts were hurled
at them, the Jagunços yelling, " Let the weakness of
the Government advance !"* and, under the brisk fire,
three or four soldiers fell.

The situation became critical.   A dangerous tremor
ran along the line, making it quiver like a snake.   A
moment more and it would have given way, and, if
it had once broken, not a man would have returned
alive.   However, in most crises, there stands out a
man to meet and dominate them.   Major Febronio,
rushing to the front, in a few moments inspired
confidence, and the exhausted, thirst-tortured soldiers
put up a brave fight.   From every side, rocks were
showered down upon them, but they were able to
stand off the Jagunços with their artillery.   A rush in

* " Avança fraqueza do governo."

superior force broke up the soldiers into groups, which still advanced to clear themselves from the defile. Little by little superior weapons carried the day, and, after a tumultuous struggle, the troops arrived upon the outskirts of the town and hurriedly encamped, after three hours of fight. The ammunition was nearly done, owing to the folly of the commander in having left so much of it behind. Still, so far, they had achieved a victory, as nearly three hundred corpses, stretched upon the ground in front of them, were there to testify. The actual losses of the troops were ten or twelve men killed and sixty wounded. The last formed a grave problem, as lack of transport forced them to be carried in rough litters, which rendered the retreat both slow and difficult. Once more their triumph was illusive, and, situated as they were, without provisions and obliged to go for water under fire, their position was most perilous, even with victory in their grasp. As soon as they had rested for an hour or two, Colonel Tamarindo held a hasty council, and put the only two alternatives that were possible before his officers. If they pushed on at daybreak and attacked the town, in the event of carrying it at once, provisions were secure; but if they failed in the face of such superior forces, and with ammunition running short, their fate was sealed, and the whole expedition would be lost.

So they decided, most unwillingly, upon retreat. All through the night there were alarms, and, when day broke, they saw they were surrounded by the enemy. Nothing remained but to break through at any cost, before starvation rendered them an easy prey to the Jagunços, who were thirsting for their blood. They observed a man, tall, bronzed and hideous, his face contracted in a savage grin, marshalling the enemy. Standing amongst a rain of bullets, he bore apparently a charmed life, and, as he passed along the ranks, a savage yell, like that raised by wild Indians, broke from his followers. This was the celebrated Pajehú, who, certainly on that occasion, confirmed his well-known courage amply, and displayed most of the qualities of a guerilla general.

As the troops were forced once more to enter the defile below Monte Cambaio to gain the open road, Pajehú reserved his main attack till they were passing underneath the rocks. There, after lining all the cliffs with sharp-shooters, he himself headed a fierce rush on the retiring troops. So impetuous was the onslaught that the Jagunços soon were mixed up with the soldiers, and fought them hand to hand. Men strove with bayonets and with knives, with cattle goads, and with clubbed rifles, all fighting for their lives. One of the Krupp guns jammed and was silenced, and Pajehú, rushing up, like a warrior of the siege of Troy, threw his arms round its muzzle, shouting to his followers to overturn it and so block up the path. The other gun, firing at short range into the sectaries who followed him, opened a passage for the troops, who, after several hours of struggle, emerged upon the plain.

Pajehú had learned a lesson, and, from that moment, the Jagunços never attempted frontal attacks upon their enemy, but put in force the tactics, ten times more efficacious, of frontier warfare—surprises, ambushes, and feints which kept the forces of the Government always in alarm, without the chance of using their superior arms. After five days of agony, quite unmolested by the enemy, tortured by hunger and by thirst, footsore and wearied out with carrying the wounded, they reached their base again. The population, who had expected that they would return victorious, saw them march through the streets in silence. Covered with dust, their arms all rusted, their helmets, often replaced by great straw hats which they had plaited hurriedly at night to shield them from the sun, with blood-stained bandages, unwashed, unshaved, and miserable, they straggled through the streets, the picture of despair. No discipline was even attempted to be preserved, and the men marched in groups supporting one another, haggard and war-worn, and at the rear followed their colonel, wounded and mounted on a mule.

So finished the much-talked-of expedition, the second that had failed before Canudos, in a lamentable style. A cry of rage ran through the country, and in the capital ministers were interpolated, and all resolved, as soon as possible, to raise a force so formidable that it was certain of success. But, far away, deep in the heart of the Sertão, after the long processions, singing hymns and carrying banners, had borne the dead towards the cemeteries, joy filled the hearts of all the sectaries.

Recruits flowed in from every side, bringing provisions with them. The trenches were extended right out to Cambaio, and all the rifles and the ammunition which the troops had left behind were carefully collected and made fit for service against the next attack. Once more the forces of the " Dog " had been defeated, owing to the efficacy of the prophet's supplications, for, during the attack, he had retired with a few faithful friends upon the beams of the half-finished church, and passed the time in prayer. When he descended and walked amongst his flock, men pressed to kiss his garment, and women, weeping as he passed, called down a blessing from on high upon their Councillor.

CHAPTER XII

In Rio de Janeiro, rage and disappointment knew no bounds, mixed, as it were, with a feeling of amazement that men undisciplined and badly armed could have defeated the best troops they had to send. They did not pause to think that the defeats had been due more to the difficulty of the country than to the rebels' arms. However, worse was still in store for them. It happened that the two defeats that the Jagunços had inflicted on the Government came at a time before it was consolidated, after the abdication of the Emperor. Several revolts had taken place in different portions of Brazil. At that time no one filled a greater space in public admiration than a certain colonel of infantry, one Antonio Moreira César, who had just returned from putting down a revolution in the south. His fame had gone before him, and he enjoyed a reputation as a brave but ferocious soldier, whose hands were steeped in blood.

Diminutive in stature, with a weak chest and bandy legs, nothing in his exterior revealed his feverish energy. His face was pale, but inexpressive, his forehead high and bulging, and over it he wore a lock of hair brought forward to conceal his baldness. His whole appearance was as that of a figure in a waxwork, and his slow gestures and halting speech completed the illusion of a low mentality. Nothing was farther from the truth. Brilliant in action, brave to temerity, he was at once patient and yet audacious in conception, a great endurer of all hardships, ambitious, revengeful, even to cruelty, but at the same time as true as steel towards the cause he had embraced.

A true production of the tropics, he passed at once from a cold reserve to a demoniac fury, having the temperament of an epileptic, for his wild fits of rage savoured of madness, though at that time it had not yet declared itself. Public opinion marked him out as the man most fitted to command against the sectaries, and, as is usually the case, public opinion showed itself favourable to the worst man for such a post. At the same time he had had great experience of frontier warfare, but in a field that differed widely from the Sertão, in the wide prairies of the south. As soon as he was named commander of the expedition he set to work with all his energy to choose his officers and make the force he had to lead so formidable as to ensure success. The Government, that could not face another check, gave him full power in everything, putting the best troops in the country at his disposition and sparing no expense. In an incredibly short time he got together thirteen hundred men, all picked from the best corps. His officers were men he could depend upon. Major Raphael Augusto Cunha Mattos commanded the artillery, which this time went well supplied with ammunition, amply sufficient for its work. The infantry was led by Captain Salomão da Rocha ; and as in the two expeditions that had failed the want of cavalry had been felt grievously, a squadron under Captain Franco was added to the force. The State militia, not great in number, but composed of men accustomed to the country and to the tactics most in use in the Sertão, was under the command of Colonel Tamarindo, who, after his disastrous retreat, was burning for revenge. Moreira César stayed but a few hours in Bahia, and at once pushed on to the railhead at Queimadas, arriving there from Rio de Janeiro, with all his forces, in the incredibly short period of five days. This exploit was to cost him dearly. Without a stop, except to leave a little garrison at Queimadas, he went on with his troops to Monte Santo, which he had chosen for his base. Hardly arrived there, either owing to his great exertions, or because the disease long dormant was now matured and ready to break out, he was seized with an epileptic fit. When he recovered he moved on to Quimguinguá, a little village on the road. There a general council of doctors and of officers was held. The doctors strongly advised delay, at least for a few days, to give Moreira César time to recover from the fit.

He overrode all opposition, and the day following, the 3rd of February, 1897, the expedition took the road under conditions more disastrous than the two previous expeditions that had failed.

This time the general was ill, the season was the most unfavourable for military operations of the whole year in the Sertão; the heat was African, the water-holes had all dried up or were reduced to mud, and all the cattle had been driven from the line of march. Most of the trees had lost their leaves in the fierce heat, a fine, red dust rose from the tracks in clouds, enveloping the soldiers in its folds, shielding the enemy's advance, and making all the trail a Calvary to the unlucky troops.

This time they determined to avoid the road by Mount Cambaio which had proved so disastrous to the previous expeditions, and after long deliberation, and seeking the advice of local men, who generally deceived them purposely both as to distances and chances of provisions on the way, they took the old trail that passed by Cumbé, Aracaty, and Rosario, though it ran through the woods. The same guide, Jesuino, now promoted to a captaincy, offered his services and was accepted with effusion, after the proofs that he had given of tried loyalty. As the road ran through woods (caatingas) it offered possibilities of shade ; but, on the other hand, the sappers had to open a path through the thick underwood, broad enough for the passage of the troops. Water was just as scarce as on the other road, and once engaged in the thick forests, they found the heat as unendurable as on the open plain. Besides all this, the trail for a long time had been abandoned by the inhabitants. Houses had been deserted, and the thick brushwood of the tropics had grown up over everything, obliterating the brief authority of man. Thus their decision was a leap into the unknown, and, after long deliberation on the advisability of carrying water in hide bags upon the mules, they rejected it, and took an Artesian field pump, and a " water searcher," who professed to know where springs were likely to be found.

By the road they saved fifty kilometres in distance ; but the difficulties that they encountered on the route wiped out completely any advantage that they had hoped to gain by the shortening of the track. Prudence of the most rudimentary order would have suggested that they should secure their base from a surprise attack when they were on the march. As on the last occasion, an over-confidence in ultimate success blinded them utterly. In Monte Santo, which in itself was open to attack, and a poor place for a prolonged defence, they left a feeble garrison of a few dozen soldiers and a quick-firing gun. Then they plunged into the unknown, without a doubt of their success, taking the forest trail.

During the three weeks that had elapsed from the defeat of Colonel Tamarindo's expedition to the launching of the next under Moreira César, Antonio Conselheiro had lost no time in strengthening his defences. The unsuccessful efforts of the Government had enormously increased his fame. Once more recruits poured in from every side, and he was able easily to fill the gaps made by the artillery amongst his followers. Extraordinary rumours of his powers soon ran like wildfire, not only through the Sertão, but in the adjoining territories. Men told each other that angels had been seen fighting in aid of the good Councillor. Others there were who swore that he himself had turned away the cannon balls with a gesture of his hand and walked unharmed amongst the thickest of the fight. Long lines of pilgrims once again toiled along the trails, bringing their cattle and good store of corn. Maimed, halt, and paralytic folk carried in hammocks by their friends arrived in numbers, mixed up with aged men and women and with cattle thieves.   All sorts and all conditions were on the move towards Canudos.   Small cattle farmers had disposed of their property to purchase arms for both themselves and for their cattle-peons. They came on their best horses, were welcomed, and at once began to prepare themselves for the ensuing fight.   Those living far away, who for some reason or another could not come themselves, sent in long trains of mules laden with corn, jerked beef, with flour, and with provisions of all kinds.   The place was thoroughly revictualled and the enthusiasm bordered on frenzy, as fresh contingents daily poured into the town.   Antonio Conselheiro multiplied himself and was seen everywhere, encouraging the men who dug the trenches, welcoming the new-comers to his Zion, and preaching fervently his doctrines of the coming ending of the world, the blessedness of suffering, and of resistance to the impious Government.

Still, he did not neglect the building of the church, employing on it all those unfit to go into the fighting line—women, and even children—coming and going to overlook their work whenever he had time.   He was determined not to be taken by surprise again, and, either having learned by past experience, or being advised by someone skilled in the art of war, he occupied all the points within a league or two outside the town to stay the enemy's advance.   Spies were sent out on every side, who penetrated easily into the bases of the Government at Monte Santo and

Queimadas, and sent him information of everything they saw.

This time, the Jagunços seem to have comprehended the folly of attacking in the open men with superior arms. Experience had taught them that their country was a natural fortress which they could make almost impregnable by the exercise of art. They dug their trenches so scientifically that it seemed almost impossible they had not been advised by a skilled captain in the art of war. At different places on the defile between Monte Cambaio and the town they erected shelters of rough stones, leaving interstices for rifle-fire, and in the trees at a convenient height they built low platforms for sharpshooters to sit on and fire upon the troops. These shelters, called in the patois of the Sertão "Mutans," they used in peace time for shooting deer, watching for tigers, or any kind of game.

Upon strategic points in the defile they heaped great rocks ready to roll on the invaders as they passed below on the one trail that led towards the town. In the great bivouac—for it was really more a bivouac than a town—the sound of preparations continued far into the night, mixed with the strains of hymns. Smiths sharpened up the swords, put a keen edge upon the knives and bayonets, tempered the scythes and cattle goads, whilst women laboured making cartridges. Powder was scarce; but in the district sulphur and saltpetre were found readily, and charcoal in a land of forests was easy to obtain. The powder that they soon produced, though rough in quality, turned out excellent. Thus, when they had

run off a store of bullets, they were ready for a siege.
Nothing was more remarkable than the frequent
arrival of bandits and of cattle thieves.   They came,
as they themselves would have said, " debaixo do
cangaço "—that is, armed cap-à-pie.   It does not
appear that they were influenced in any way by hopes
of plunder or of gain, for on arrival they all submitted
cheerfully to the discipline imposed by the town
commander, João Abbade, who turned them into
improvised non-commissioned officers, giving them
posts to hold.

When all is said, it is impossible not to sympathise
to some extent with the misguided sectaries, for all
they wanted was to live the life they had been
accustomed to, and sing their litanies. Clearly Antonio
Conselheiro had no views on any subject under heaven
outside his own district. His dreams were fixed upon
a better world, and his chief care to fit his followers
for the change that he believed was to take place
so soon.

As usual in all times of difficulty, he fell back on
more religious ceremonies, more litanies, more self-
abasement, and longer periods of fasting and of penitence that he enjoined on all.   His spies returned—
bringing accurate information, both of the number
and the power of his foes. So much they talked of
the death-dealing guns, the regiments of well-armed
troops, and of the terror of Moreira César's name,
that the simple people dubbed him " Anti-Christ,"
thinking he was the awful being whom they heard
so much about from their good Councillor. For
the first time in their long trials their faith was

shaken for a space; not that they feared to die for the cause they had espoused, but feared to lose their lives too soon, before the prophecies that they had heard from Conselheiro had been accomplished, and thus to forfeit the kingdom of the saints that he had promised them.

A great procession that they made to the new church, and a fierce sermon from the Councillor, promising victory, restored their spirits, and they prepared themselves to fight, right to the bitter end. A few deserted, but their desertions only revived the fervour of the rest. Antonio Conselheiro (after his preparations for defence were made) ordained a day of prayer and of humiliation. Long trains of women dressed in black converged upon the church. The faithful thronged its aisles. Then, in dead silence, he ascended to the pulpit, and, looking out upon his flock, instead of launching into a perfervid oration, bowed his head, and fixed his eyes upon the ground for a considerable space. Lifting his head once more, he turned his macerated countenance towards the faithful, and in a broken phrase or two implored God's blessing on them all. The effect was magical and instantaneous. Hope once again revived, and with a shout of "Death to Anti-Christ!" the congregation poured out of the church and each man sought his post.

CHAPTER XIII

Upon his side Moreira César had not been idle, but had done all he could to get his troops up to a high state of efficiency. On the 22nd of February he held a review at Monte Santo, and found he had twelve hundred and eighty men of all arms, including fifty cavalry. Each man had two hundred and fifty cartridges provided for him, and these were carried either in cartridge belts or packed up on the mules. Besides all this, a train of pack-mules and a few waggons followed with the baggage, and sixty thousand cartridges. A battery of four Krupp guns, commanded by Captain da Rocha, made a brave show at the review. Major Raphael Augusto da Cunha Mattos and Colonel Tamarindo, both anxious for revenge for their past reverses, each had commands they took up eagerly.

So the stage was set for a minor action in the great drama that has been going on for centuries between the old world, and what was the new order, up to yesterday. In the days of Antonio Conselheiro, the challenge of the Semitico-Asiatic hordes had not been sounded, and the security of life and property, with European marriage, all seemed as firmly rooted as the foundations of the world.

After the review was over, instead of dismissing

his men to their tents and bivouacs, Moreira César
sounded the advance to the astonishment of everybody,
and the whole expedition left Monte Santo an hour
or two before the dark.   In three days they reached
Cumbé, after a journey even more painful than those
the first two expeditions had endured.   The full force
of the drought now had reigned for the whole
summer in the Sertão.   In places where there had
been water-holes, none now were to be found.   The
trees stood up gaunt skeletons, looking like sign-posts
on the road to ruin.   The very birds had long deserted
the thirst-tortured country.   Cattle had all been
driven off to better pasturage.   Even the rare wild
beasts that crossed the column on the route, wild-cats
and jaguars, were thin and mangy, and looked desperate with thirst.   The soldiers fired at them in a
perfunctory way, but failed to hit them, and the beasts
appeared to grin and mock at them as they snarled at
the puffs of sand the bullets threw up near their path.
Only the lizards seemed at home and basked upon the
heated stones like salamanders.   The glare from
heaven met the heat ascending from the parched earth,
and the soldiers fancied they had entered purgatory.
After Cumbé, hoping to escape attack, the expedition
this time left the forests on their right, following the
road by Cajazeiras and Serra Branca in the plains, but
passing underneath a range of hills.   The guides pro-
tested at the choice of route, saying it was the hottest
and most desolate in the whole Sertão ; but Moreira
César overruled them, and, on his horse, headed the
column under a sun that seemed to petrify the brains.
After an eight hours' march, the exhausted men, who

had not drunk a drop of water all day long, arrived at
Serra Branca.   The General slipped exhausted from
his horse, that hung its head, too tired even to whisk
its tail to keep the flies away.   The men let themselves fall down in the ranks and lay, with their
tongues blackened with thirst, hanging out of their
mouths, like dogs after a long day's work.

Their first care, after a little rest, was to set up the
Artesian pump, but, to their horror, they discovered
that instead of packing up with it a borer for the
necessary holes, a machine for raising weights had by
some accident been substituted.   Nothing remained
but to wait till nightfall brought relief from the per-
secuting sun, and then march on again.   Marching
all night, stumbling and falling in the darkness, the
men up to their knees in the deep, sandy road, at last,
just before daybreak, they reached Rosario, where
there was a well.

Fevered, and having passed full sixteen hours
athirst, after a night almost as cold as the day was
tropical, the soldiers drank till it seemed they would
exhaust the well.   Fortunately all South Americans,
whether of Spanish or Portuguese extraction, are
patient under suffering, and endure hardships under
which European troops would sink.   In a short time,
after a sleep and rest, all were restored to spirits and
congratulated themselves on having passed their night
of misery without an enemy attack.   Fires burned on
the horizon, and now and then during the night they
fancied shadowy figures had accompanied the expedition, at a little distance from their ranks.   These may
have been creations of their sun-heated brains, or spies of

the Jagunços, who seem to have comprehended that the climate and the hardships of the route were just as efficacious aids against their enemies as a resort to arms. Their system was apparently to lure the soldiers as far as possible into their territory, for the third expedition never was attacked upon the road.

The soldiers' spirits rose, and a slight rainfall that lasted half an hour refreshed their bodies, so that they began once more to despise their enemy, and talk of a mere military promenade, after the fashion of the expeditions that had preceded them upon their journey towards defeat. Once more the rain descended, this time with fury, turning the roads to rivers of liquid mud, and making all manœuvres difficult. The order to break camp was given just at daylight, and, in the gloom and rain, the soldiers struck their tents. An alarm was sounded suddenly, but proved fallacious, and on the 1st of March they once more set out on their way. On the 3rd, they camped at a place called Pitombas, after a stage of seven or eight leagues. The rain had ceased, and in an hour or two the sun once more was their chief enemy.

Already they had arrived close to Canudos without attack, or the least sign, except the furtive figures in the night of the Jagunços spying on them. As they marched on, singing in the ranks, the soldiers talked of an easy victory. With such a chief as was Moreira César, all things were possible. Some spoke of break-fasting next day inside Canudos, and others openly lamented that they would be obliged to go back without a combat or without a cartridge spent. From one end to the other of the long, straggling line ran

jokes and gasconades, whilst many wondered why so
many admirable strategic points had been left un-
defended by the enemy.   In fact, once more they fell
into the old mistake of over-confidence, not compre-
hending the tactics of Antonio Conselheiro in luring
them into the lion's den.   Just as they left Pitombas,
to march on to the last stage at Angico where they
proposed to camp, a fusillade, from a belt of bush,
caused them to stand to arms.   At the first fire from
the unseen enemy, they lost an officer and six or seven
men.   Moreira César ordered a halt and threw out
skirmishers.   These advanced, firing into the bush.
All that they saw was the opening and closing of the
scrub, as the Jagunços disappeared into the woods.

They found a shot-gun lying on the ground, and
this they brought to their commander as the spoils of
victory.   Taking it in one hand, he fired it off into
the air, remarking tranquilly, " Their arms are quite
inefficacious and little to be feared."   He little knew
what was in store for him.

The wounded men he left in Pitombas with a
doctor and a guard, and pushed on rapidly.   Instead
of stopping at Angico to rest his soldiers, as a prudent
soldier would have done, taking full time to lay his
plans and hear his scouts' reports, he only stayed a
quarter of an hour.   Riding to the head of the
column, he addressed his men.   " Comrades," he said,
" you see my health is bad ; a man can die but once ;
but after all our goal Canudos is quite close to us.
Let us advance and capture it at once."

The soldiers answered him with cheers.   " Yes,
General," they cried, " we will all follow you.   Let

us push on at once." After six hours of a most painful march, they reached the little hill called Mount Favella, and, passing round it, saw Canudos at their feet. Rapidly bringing up a gun, the artillerymen fired two rounds, and Moreira César, with a smile, remarked, "There go two visiting cards for Antonio Conselheiro, to tell him I am here."

Why, having four Krupp guns with him, he did not send a message to Antonio Conselheiro, to tell him that he must surrender, or have the place blown to pieces, is difficult to understand. After the fashion of the other commanders of former expeditions, he seems to have grossly undervalued the Jagunços' fighting powers. Instead of opening fire in a serious way, he limited himself to his two "visiting cards," and then encamped his men. It was the more extraordinary as the two shots fired, almost in sport, set on fire several houses, making the soldiers laugh as they saw the inhabitants scurrying in confusion to a place of safety in the rear of the great church. After a brief rest in the encampment that dominated all the town, at one o'clock the troops advanced to the attack, thinking no doubt that in an hour they would be masters of the place. Moreira César does not seem to have had the faintest doubt of a success. So he advanced his men in column with the artillery upon the flanks, and marched straight into the labyrinth of winding streets without a qualm, amidst a silence of the tomb. The men pushed on, their ranks a little broken by the winding lanes, laughing and joking, exclaiming, as they found the houses all deserted, "This is a city of the dead." When the last files had entered the intricate system of lanes and counterlanes, suddenly a hot fire broke out upon them from behind houses, from rifle-pits, artfully covered up with palm-leaves, and from the high walls of the unfinished church. From every side, from underground and from the sky, as it appeared, shots fell into them, doing considerable execution, and causing almost a panic in the ranks. Nothing remained but to retreat at once or take the houses and dislodge the sharpshooters, at the bayonet's point. The soldiers, though taken by surprise, soon rallied bravely, and rushed to the attack. As they advanced, more rifle-pits were discovered in their rear, and they were caught between two fires.

The winding streets that often ran into "deadends," causing a charge to turn when it found its way barred to it, soon broke the attacking force into small groups that advanced upon the houses and the riflepits, separated from the main body of the troops. The artillery was afraid to fire, for soon the whole vast, human warren was alive with struggles, in which men fought without the slightest order, with bayonets, with rifle butts, and knives. In the fierce mêlée, all the advantage of discipline was lost, and the athletic Sertanejos were more experienced in fighting of that nature than the individual soldiers of the troops. Shots were fired at the ranks point blank, from rifles thrust through the interstices of the rudely built houses, and never failed to find their mark. Women, wild-eyed, and with their hair all streaming in the wind, loaded the old-fashioned blunderbusses as fast as they were emptied, or brought up others ready charged to put into the hands

of the fierce combatants. They carried bags of cartridges for the modern weapons, for, by this time,
either by purchase or taken from the dead of the past
expeditions, a number of good rifles had fallen into
the Jagunços' hands. As the doomed soldiers advanced
farther into the town, all kinds of projectiles were
showered upon them: hot water, stones heated in the
fire, and torches made of rope dipped in tar fell thickly
on their heads. When the troops took a group of
houses, not without serious losses to themselves, they
tore them down, only to find another group, equally
well defended, just in front of them. During the
battle psalmody was heard, long and lugubrious, a
trailing melody of sound, that made itself distinctly
audible through all the firing and the noise.

The soldiers raised their heads involuntarily, and
saw, to their amazement, the prophet, with a dozen of
his men, standing on the walls of the great church,
singing their litanies as composedly as if no combat
was in progress and no fight was going on. A rain
of bullets failed to reach him, and the lugubrious
strains were turned into a hymn of triumph; and still
the fight surged wildly in the streets, with varying
success.

Numbers began to tell, and, by degrees, the exhausted soldiers were forced back again towards the
outskirts of the town. A prudent leader would have
sounded a retreat and started fire with his artillery.
Moreira César, though a brave man, experienced in
war, was rash to a degree and over-confident. So,
getting on his horse, he placed himself at the head of
his small troop of cavalry to lead a charge into the

town. They did not number more than fifty, and all their horses either were lame or out of condition for a charge, through dint of travelling. At a hand gallop they advanced, Moreira César riding at their head and brandishing his sword. A brook spread out between them and the town, and, as they galloped down the slope to cross its channel, several of the tired and worn-out horses fell, crushing their riders and breaking up the ranks. Just in the middle of the stream they were exposed to a hot fire from hidden rifle-pits. Saddles were emptied, the charge weakened and broke, and then a panic seized upon the men, who turned to flee, all in confusion, an easy target to the hidden riflemen. Moreira César, mad with distress and shame, galloped furiously about, shouting and cursing in an attempt to turn the fugitives. Just as he gained the bank, a bullet struck him in the stomach, and he dropped his reins, exclaiming, "It is nothing," though his head fell down upon his breast.

Two officers spurred to his side, seeing his situation, but, as they reached him, and were stretching out their hands, a second bullet hit him, this time mortally. Still he remained upon his horse, supported on each side by his two officers, who brought him, still seated half-unconscious in the saddle, back to the encampment that he so recently had left.

The command devolved on Colonel Tamarindo, who, with more prudence than his chief, set about instantly to disengage his forces from the town, and to re-form his scattered companies under the fire of the artillery.

Night was just falling as the troops slowly disengaged themselves out of the labyrinth. The Angelus rang out, and, as it sounded in the now silent air, the fierce Jagunços threw their leather hats upon the ground, crossed themselves piously, and, falling on their knees, prayed fervently, thanking the God of Battles, who, at the intercession of their Councillor, had sent them victory.

CHAPTER XIV

WHEN at last Colonel Tamarindo had withdrawn his troops out of the hornet's nest into which the rashness of their late chief had plunged them, he fell back upon his guns. By this time all the ranks were broken, and though the troops had inflicted heavy losses on the enemy, their own, in ratio to their numbers, were still heavier. The little hill on which the guns were placed was too close to the town for them to stay there, for fear of a surprise. Therefore, in a confused and mixed-up mass, they retreated to a higher hill called Alto do Mario, four or five hundred yards away. There they encamped in a roughly formed square, with their artillery and baggage animals inside of it. As several hours of light remained, why they did not at once reduce the town to ruins with their four Krupp guns has never been explained.

Moreira César, though rash and ill-advised, was above all a man of energy. Had he been fit to take the leadership, all yet might have been saved, and discipline once more established in the ranks. His successor, Colonel Tamarindo, although a man accustomed to adventures from his youth, and trained in frontier fighting, broken to hardships, and a brave officer, was yet a fatalist. Perhaps disheartened by

his previous defeat, or from his age, for he had long
passed sixty, he had set out upon the expedition quite
against his will. From the first day he had been
melancholy, and now, just at the moment when he
had to take command, he fell into a fit of stupor, and,
sitting down upon a box, rested his head between his
hands. Nothing could move him from his lethargy.
To the officers who came to him to ask instructions
all he would reply was, " Do the best you can under
the circumstances." This attitude completed their
discouragement. It was the moment for a man of
spirit to curse a little, to pray a little, to talk of
honour and of home, of sweethearts and of wives ; to
strike some, half in anger, half playfully with the flat
of his sword, to encourage falterers with a brave
word, to curb the headstrong, and by example, bring
back courage into their hearts and order to the ranks.
Poor Colonel Tamarindo was not the man for the
plight in which they found themselves. His officers
must have thought with regret upon their rash but
energetic chief, mortally wounded, lying helpless in
an old ruined house called " A Fazenda Velha," in
the middle of the square.

Night fell upon the beaten and discouraged men,
as it so often falls in the Sertão, starlit and silent. The
stars shone out like moons in the clear atmosphere,
and just above Canudos, the Southern Cross rose
slowly till it appeared to be on watch above the city
of the Councillor. Every few minutes flashes of
summer lightning illuminated everything, making the
night still more mysterious in the interval. Frogs
croaked with a metallic note, cicalas chirped, and in

the scanty bushes on the river bank myriads of fire-
flies, looking like a shower of golden spangles, twinkled
and darted to and fro.   Such nights appear to bring
the soul into more intimate connection with the spirit
of Nature, and lift it out of the region of mere selfish
yearnings to be one with God, for its own welfare,
into communion, not only with the Deity, but with
all that He has made.

Little enough did the disorganised mass of soldiery
think of such matters, and their immediate care was
for their lives.   A hurried council of the chief officers
was held by the camp fire, and after short delibera-
tions they agreed to acquaint their dying leader that
they had resolved upon retreat.   A captain was de-
puted to convey the news to him as he lay with his
head upon a saddle, wrapped in his military cloak.
Though he had but a few more hours of life, his head
was clear, clearer perhaps than it had been throughout
the course of the disastrous expedition, and his resolution fixed and unchangeable.   He heard the message
with amazement.   Then raising himself on one elbow,
pale, and with the dews of death upon his hair, but
resolute and energetic to the last, in a clear voice he
gave his reasons against their policy.

"We have," he said, "seven or eight hundred
soldiers still remaining, all armed and well-supplied
with ammunition.   It is your duty to restore discipline amongst them, and this once done, there are
enough of them to carry on the fight.   Our position
here is good, for with our guns we dominate the
town.   Attack it boldly and it will be yours."   From
reasoning he passed on to reproach, to fury, and to

despair, but could not put his courage and his resolution into hearts dead to shame. Then he gave his last order. " This retreat is not to be begun." This did not move them. So, calling for his secretary, he dictated to him his last dispatch, telling the Government of all that he had done. Lastly, broken by fast approaching death and shame at the retreat that he saw would be begun as soon as he no longer had the power to give an order or protest, in his own hand he wrote upon the margin of the document, " I retire from the army." Then sinking back upon the ground, he wrapped his head up in his cloak, and in a few hours passed away without a word.

His death completed the confusion and despair of his discouraged troops. In addition to the difficulties of their position and to the distance that they had to go before they possibly could reach a place of safety, a wave of superstition now swept over all of them. The over-confidence with which they had set out, and the ill-judged contempt of an enemy not to be despised, had given way to a blind terror of him. The soldiers all came from the northern provinces, and in essentials, though with a tinge of negro blood, were of the same race as their enemies. The name of Antonio Conselheiro was familiar to them. Most likely all had heard of, and some believed in, his supernatural powers. Amongst the ranks there was no stiffening of better educated men from near the capital. The energetic Paulistas* were conspicuous by their absence, and none of the Rio Grande men, themselves half Gauchos, and accustomed to inter-

* Men from São Paulo.

course with the materialistic Gauchos of Uruguay and of the Argentine, were there to mock their fears. Wild stories circulated about Antonio Conselheiro's powers. He had been seen, alone, high on the church, catching the bullets in his hands, and dropping them upon the ground. All that had happened seemed inexplicable to the superstitious soldiers, and most of all, the defeat and death of their commander, whom they all looked on as invincible. At midnight the whole camp was thrown into alarm. The sentinels and scouts came in, firing their rifles as they ran. Up from Canudos, buried in the depths of darkness, came a sound of many voices, a hum as of advancing thousands, so it appeared to them. They stood to arms, and listened, then their vain terrors were accentuated, for it was not the sound of an advancing host that had alarmed them, but a universal prayer. Women and men and children, old and young, combatants and non-combatants alike, were praying fervently, led by the prophet from the highest point of vantage on the half-finished church.

It was a sound that must to anyone have seemed mysterious, even terrifying. A town of possibly some twenty thousand souls all praying with one voice and one accord, out of the darkness of the night. To the half-beaten, wholly shaken soldiery grouped listening on the hill, it sent a thrill of superstitious terror that penetrated to their souls. Victory was still within their grasp had they but known it, or had a particle of the energy of poor Moreira César, now lying dead, wrapped in his military cloak—the fittest winding sheet of a brave soldier—possessed their officers. Their strength was in the guns that they had failed to use, and by whose aid the wretched village at their feet was dominated. No weapons can give courage to a coward, and in their case the ancient Spanish saying, "Weighed down with iron, weighed down with fear"* was amply verified.

The first faint streaks of dawn saw them all ready for the road. Their leader, Colonel Tamarindo, now in some part emerged from the stupor that had overwhelmed him, had the sense left to marshal all his men into some sort of order for their arduous retreat. The first to leave the ground was a detachment of the best troops, and what remained of the defeated cavalry. These he threw out upon his wings to act as scouts ; but the disabled condition of their horses that had passed a night deprived of water and of food detracted from their use.

Then came the vanguard, escorting all the baggage animals, and with the wounded carried in litters, roughly improvised ; then, wrapped in a hide, the body of their leader, lashed upon a mule. Lastly came half ot the artillery, for they had left two of their guns under a subaltern upon the hill on which the camp had been erected, with orders to delay the enemy's advance at any cost.

This he did bravely, for at the moment that the last files of the retreating troops left the encampment, he was attacked on every side. A bell on the great church called everyone to arms down in Canudos, and from all sides a hot discharge broke on the brave young officer and his artillerymen. When he judged

* " Cargado de hierro, cargado de miedo."

that his comrades had begun their march in safety, and after having killed almost a hundred of the enemy, he withdrew his guns, retreating in good order, after the retiring force.   Had he but stayed and turned his guns upon the town, the whole result of the disastrous expedition might have been altered; but it was written otherwise in the great book of human folly which so many take for fate.

When the day broke, it showed the column on the march, still in good order, but outflanked on every side by the Jagunços, who from the points of vantage on the road poured in a galling fire.   Still there was nothing in their situation that an energetic leader could not have coped with, had but some discipline been kept, and the most elementary knowledge of conducting a retreat existed anywhere.   Once clear of the defiles, and in the plains, they might have camped beside a river, grazed their pack animals under a guard, whilst the artillery held back the enemy till all were rested, and an orderly retreat was entered on. This by degrees would have brought them all to safety, for the Jagunços never ventured far from their own territory.

Nothing was farther from the minds of the mulatto soldiers than to make a stand.   Their comrades were falling in the ranks at every volley the Jagunços fired. Only the artillery bringing up the rear resisted, firing bravely into the thick ranks of the pursuing sectaries. Little by little the artillerymen were picked off by the sharpshooters, falling beside their guns.   They all fell bravely, with their faces to the foe.

Their fate, and the reluctance of the Jagunços to

close in upon them, shows clearly what might have been accomplished, had but the rest of the retreating expedition shown ordinary nerve.   At last the catastrophe burst on the retreating horde.   The guns, which had been dragged by mules, stopped suddenly at a corner of the road before the retreating expedition had disengaged itself from the defile below Monte Cambaio.   Colonel Tamarindo, who since the break of day had manifested an energy and a courage in inverse ratio to his weakness of the night before, exposed his life recklessly, galloping fearlessly from one end of the column to the other, trying to infuse some spirit in his men.   His efforts all were useless, and the last artillerymen were slaughtered round their guns.   With shouts of triumph the Jagunços closed in, with overwhelming numbers on the column.   It made but slight resistance; but abandoning the baggage animals, leaving the body of Moreira César on the ground, all broke into a mad flight.   Knapsacks and guns were cast away.   Bayonets and cartridge cases, blankets and greatcoats littered the road on every side. Like vultures the Jagunços swooped down on the deserted guns, cutting down Capitan Salomão and four brave artillerymen, who remained faithful to the end.

Colonel Tamarindo, left alone, still tried to stay the tide of fugitives, displaying a courage and contempt of death which he had brought too late into the field. As he was galloping, waving his sword and shouting orders to the flying men, a bullet struck him in the breast.   He fell, half dying, and to an officer who galloped up to him gave his last order with his failing breath,   " I leave the command to Colonel Cunha

Mattos "; then he rolled between the feet of his expiring horse, that, pierced with twenty bullets, had staggered up against a rock.

The expedition, which such a little time ago had left its base well-armed and well-provisioned, confident of success, marching to the sound of bugle and of drum, had disappeared. All that remained was a mere mob of fugitives. Eight hundred men, without provisions, defenceless, burning with thirst, helpless and deprived of guides, were left like shipwrecked mariners tossed without compass on the sea. Many who left the roads soon lost their way, and perished in the woods of hunger and of thirst. About five hundred kept together, unpursued, for the Jagunços were occupied in dragging back the guns, in hunting up the mules laden with ammunition and provisions, and in picking up the rifles, bayonets, and arms that they found strewn upon the ground. The store of ammunition which Moreira César had left behind at O Rosario all fell into the hands of the triumphant sectaries, who thus were able to equip the front ranks of their fighting line with better weapons, which they used with considerable effect against their enemies.

After three days of agonising flight, in which men dropped upon the sand and died at every turning of the road, the main group of the fugitives reached Monte Santo unpursued, except by their own fears. What they underwent upon the road, without provisions, in the full rigour of the summer, forced to struggle on continuously, or else to die of thirst, can be more easily imagined than described. In the striking phrase of Euclydes da Cunha,* which in itself was taken from the Jagunços, " the forces of the Government had become a weakness,"† for the time being, at the least.   All the result of the expedition, under the much vaunted leader, Moreira César, had been to equip the Jagunços for the first time with artillery, and with a plentiful supply of arms.   It had also stimulated their fanaticism, and raised the prestige of Antonio Conselheiro to an unprecedented height. His followers looked on their victory as a miracle brought about by his prayers.   They had seen the forces of the Government arrive before Canudos, at the first fire of the artillery set several houses burning, and had given themselves up for lost.   Then, without apparent reason, they had seen the same forces, still unbroken, still with their formidable artillery covering their retreat, retire and break into disorder, then turn into a rabble and throw their arms upon the ground. What wonder that to ignorant and superstitious men it seemed a miracle ?

Their unlooked-for victory seems to have stirred up in their minds instincts that perhaps they owed to their remotest ancestors in Africa, or to the Tupi Indians, whose blood flowed in the veins of many of them.   After the battle and the collecting of the arms, they next turned their attention to the dead. These they decapitated, and burned the bodies in great piles.   The heads they placed on stakes on each side of the defile between Canudos and Mount

* " Os Sertoẽs."

† A play upon the words " força," force, and " fraqueza," weakness.

Cambaiao, just as the Ashantis had an avenue of heads before their capital. Above each head, upon the trees and bushes, was hung a knapsack, a jacket, or a kepi, a belt, a saddle, or a military cloak, so that the whole road seemed a rag-fair, of death.

Lastly, impaled and standing upright, shrivelled to a mummy in the dry air of the Sertão, they stuck the body of Colonel Tamarindo, as if he still commanded his unlucky men, placing it only a yard or two from where he fell. His horse, mortally wounded, had staggered a few paces farther on before it died upon its feet, resting against a bank. The Jagunços left it where it had finished its career, and the dry climate desiccated it, so that months afterwards, when a new expedition passed through the defile, it was still perfect, undecayed and dry, with the wind lifting up its mane occasionally—a veritable pale horse of death, descended lineally from its prototype in the Apocalypse.

CHAPTER XV

FOR the third time the forces of the Government had suffered a reverse, at the hands of men undisciplined, ill-armed, and aided chiefly by the difficulties of the country where they lived. There was no compromise possible to be arrived at between the forces that were engaged. The Government could not afford to treat in any way with Antonio Conselheiro, for they had nothing in their power to offer him. He on his side, most likely, would never have consented to hold a parley with the entity that he had typified as Anti-Christ.

The blow that the Government had received was grievous to its prestige, unstable as it was, with several revolutions on its hands. Still, they were not so serious as the movement in the Sertão, as they were of the kind common in South America, raised by ambitious men. Had any of them triumphed, one Government would have succeeded another, very like the last. Antonio Conselheiro, with his millenniary doctrine, challenged, even if he was unaware of it himself, all the foundations of society. No challenge is so fatal to any system as to predict its speedy ending, for at once the state of things so challenged becomes of no account to the believers in the prophecy.

Antonio Conselheiro probably had no very definite ideas either of his own position or of the power of the Government. His late success does not appear to have elated him unduly, nor did he seem to have conceived any ideas of conquest beyond the limits of the Sertão.

Had he been let alone, it is probable that things would have gone on quite quietly, for his doctrines seem to have been quite fitted to his followers. There being no accommodation possible between a Government that held the usual comfortable doctrine that to-morrow will be the same as yesterday, and heralded all change as progress, being quite positive that they were the repository of all wisdom and all common sense, and on the other hand a prophet who esteemed all worldly wisdom a mere tinkling cymbal, nothing was left but to fight out the question to the end. This was what both sides were prepared to do.

The Government assembled in Bahia a force of some five thousand men, with field and siege artillery, half a regiment of cavalry from Rio Grande do Sul, composed of Gauchos, the whole under the command of General Arthur Oscar de Andrade Guimaraens, an officer of considerable renown.

Once more the vainglorious and foolish over-confidence that had proved so disastrous to the three previous expeditions overtook the fourth. The General's orders were to lose as little time as possible in Bahia, but to push on at once to the railhead at Queimadas, and there establish a provisional base of operations, and await the arrival of more troops. This he was forced to do, even more speedily than he had bargained for, by the foolish conduct of his officers and men.

The officers, mostly cadets, just through the military schools, who probably had never left the capital, saw in Bahia only an advanced post of the Sertão. The winding streets and high colonial houses with their red-tiled roofs, the wealth of convents and of churches, dark passages and massive doors with coats-of-arms cut deeply over them, only appeared to the young men as vestiges of barbarism. They went about, clanking their sabres, trailing their useless spurs upon the pavements, and going on as if they were in occupation of a conquered territory. They all affected to perceive in the revolt of the Jagunços a movement to restore the monarchy. Hardly a day passed without some disagreeable incident, or some collision with the civil population, who were as much opposed to Antonio Conselheiro as were the officers themselves.

The General was obliged to issue orders that the troops should entrain for Queimadas, straight from the harbour, so that in a few days, after having left a disagreeable feeling in Bahia, all were assembled at the railhead, and marched on without delay to Monte Santo, which as before was chosen for the base.

Antonio Conselheiro seems to have had little or no illusions as to the fate reserved for him and for the Zion of his followers, in the face of such a formidable force. Nevertheless, he made all preparations for a desperate defence. The great new church was almost finished by this time. On it he mounted two of the Krupp guns taken from the third expedition. The other two he placed in strategic positions to guard the

approaches to the town. People still flowed towards
Canudos, bringing provisions with them, and the
whole country to his rear was open to him, and in
the main favourable to his cause. He now disposed
of a certain quantity of modern rifles and a good
store of ammunition for them.

The spiritual appeal he in nowise neglected, preaching incessantly, enjoining even more rigorous fasting
and penitence, prophesying the final judgment, after
the reign of Don Sebastian upon earth. Whether
the leaders who were steeped in crime, as Pajehú and
Macambira, believed in, or even cared about the
coming of an illusory King to reign in glory and to
judge the world previous to its destruction, is a moot
point, for who shall dive into the mysteries of the
human mind or search its follies? Perhaps they had
a vague belief, or were impressed by Antonio Conselheiro, accustomed as they all were to the outward
forms of the Catholic religion from their infancy.
Most likely they felt rather than reasoned out that
the wild life in the Sertão would be ended if the
Government should conquer, and they themselves
subjected to the law. At any rate, they gave un-
questioning obedience to their leader, and did their
utmost to prepare for the death-struggle that awaited
them.

Upon the other side, the railhead at Queimadas
rang with the din of preparations. A great instruc-
tion camp was formed, and on its parade-ground the
soldiers trained incessantly, practising such evolutions
as appeared best suited to a campaign in the Sertão.
Warned by experience, the General had a regiment of

scouts dressed in the leather clothes of the Jagunços, making it possible for them to manœuvre in the bush. The body of the troops, unluckily for them, still kept their gaudy uniforms, rendering them an easy mark for the sharpshooters who annoyed them on the march. Two months were thus consumed in preparations, giving the soldiers time to become discontented with their monotonous surroundings, and in some degree infected by the inhabitants with a vague terror of the enemy. The rank-and-file were almost all men drawn from the northern provinces, accustomed from their earliest years to hear of miracles performed by various impostors, or self-deceivers, who from time to time appeared. Most likely many of them saw nothing improbable in the coming of the King, Don Sebastian, to reign upon the earth. By race and training, and by the ties of superstition and of faith, they were not far removed from the Jagunços whom they were called upon to fight. Their discontent was rendered more acute by scarcity of food, for the commissariat, hastily organised and badly planned, had proved a failure. Flour soon was finished, and the troops depended for their food upon the thin cattle which were driven down to them through grassless districts, arriving famishing and travel-worn.

The situation in Queimadas was disastrous. The armies of the republic, but just emerged from a long revolutionary struggle, were in confusion. Only a single line existed to the coast. By it the troops, the ammunition and provisions, all filtered slowly up towards the base. When regiments arrived, the greater part of them were far below their strength

on paper, and half were raw recruits.   Orders were
sent from Rio de Janeiro to march at once, and to
secure success if possible; for the Government had
suffered seriously by the three previous blows.   The
General, Arthur Oscar, adopted a plan for his attack
almost precisely similar to that adopted by Moreira
César, with the exception that his forces were far
larger and his artillery much more formidable.   Two
columns, one under General Silva Barbosa, and the
other commanded by General Savaget, were to converge upon the town.   Given the circumstances and
the nature of the country, it is difficult to see what
other plan could have been hit upon.   To make
things more secure General Arthur Oscar added a
third column to attack Canudos in the rear.   Pushed
by the Government, and compelled to make a show of
great activity, he sent off General Savaget, early in
April, with a column, by the Joazeiro-Villa Nova
road.   He himself was detained, by the need to train
his raw recruits, by shortness of provisions and by the
lack of ammunition for his guns, until the end of
June.   During this interval the discontent amongst
the troops at the inaction and the want of food
became so great, that in order to appease it a
hypothetical reconnaissance was undertaken towards
the insurgents' outworks at the strategic points.   This
expedient, so well known to leaders in a like position,
nearly ended in a catastrophe, owing to the rashness
of Colonel Thompson Flores, the colonel in command.

This officer, unused to frontier warfare, and jealous
of the luck, as he considered it, of General Savaget,
who he imagined would take Canudos with a rush,

determined to push on, and to win laurels on his own account.   Only an urgent dispatch from headquarters saved him from rushing on his fate.   Nothing appears to have served as a lesson sharp enough to make the Brazilian national troops aware of the great difficulties of a campaign in the Sertão.   They all appeared to think that in the familiar Spanish phrase, " They could arrive and kiss the saint,"* unaware, perhaps, that the twin paths that lead to heaven and glory are arduous to tread.

Towards the end of June (1897) General Arthur Oscar gave the signal to depart.   The ill-trained, half-starved troops plunged into the wilderness upon half rations—not a good preparation for a difficult campaign.   With them they took a large siege gun, a Whitworth, that weighed nearly two thousand pounds.†   This piece of ordnance put the expedition to great trouble, for transport animals were scarce, roads were non-existent, and in the month of June such tracks as did exist were ankle-deep in mud.   The General seems to have imagined that he had to embark upon a semi-European style of warfare, and so annoyed his troops with a strict discipline as to formation on the march. The heavy Whitworth gun, with a battery of Krupp fieldpieces and half a dozen quick-firers, made an imposing show.   A corps of sappers had to go in front to prepare the way for it, levelling the track in places, constructing bridges at the streams, and gener- ally losing time.   Of the three roads that lead towards Canudos, two, those of Cambaiao and Massacara, had

* " Llegar y besar al santo."
† Euclydes da Cunha, " Os Sertoës," p. 377.

been rendered almost transitable by the expeditions that had failed. Their worst asperities had been levelled down and their strategic points were known. The third road that led by Calumby was the shortest of the three, and the least difficult. This road the Jagunços had fortified so strongly that it would have been impossible to force. Therefore the expedition avoided it, passing to the eastward under the slopes of Mont Aracaty, and following more or less the track of the first expedition that had essayed the task.

Of all the expeditions, the fourth, encumbered as it was with a full military train, advanced the slowest. Four or five painful days upon the road brought them into the danger zone at the Lagoa da Lage, where for the first time they had a skirmish with the enemy. By the 26th, they only had advanced eighty kilometres from Monte Santo upon their painful road. At times, in order to avoid marshy places where the big gun would certainly have sunk, they had to cut a path for a mile or two through the thick bush, a perfect labyrinth of thorns.

Colonel Siqueira de Menezes, who accompanied the expedition, in an article to the newspaper *O Paiz*, of Rio, has preserved the names of some of the most thorny plants, as Chique-Chique, Palmatorio, Rabo de Raposa,* Mundacarús, Croás, Cabeça de Frade,† and many more, whose designations are as terrific as the most thorny of the thorns.

From this time forward the expedition was continuously attacked. Ambushes by day, alarms by night, attempts to stampede the baggage animals,

* Fox's tail.   † Friar's head.

succeeded one another, giving the troops no rest. Arrived at the ill-fated position of Angico, they passed along the deep, worn path, between thick bush, where the heads of those decapitated by the Jagunços, after the rout of the third expedition, were all stuck up on stakes. It seemed to the raw troops that they had entered on the road to hell, so great their horror was, as the wind swayed some of the mummied bodies, which had been fastened to the trees, in a fantastic dance.

Lastly, they came upon the body of 'Colonel Tamarindo, still with black gloves upon the hands, the decapitated head hung from a branch above it, and a little farther on, his horse, still on its feet against the bank, with its mane waving in the breeze. As they were passing the defile, guarded by the dry bodies of their former comrades, Pajehú attacked in force, but hidden by the bush. A rain of bullets fell amongst the troops marching in close formation, and in a moment there were many casualties inflicted by the unseen enemy. The quick-firing guns enabled them to beat back the attack, and in the evening they arrived at Monte Favella that overlooked the town.

The expedition camped in the valley underneath the hill. From the low hill, the General and his Staff gazed down with wonder on the town. Was this the place—a mere assemblage of mud-huts that looked so fragile that it seemed a push would throw them on the ground—that had foiled three expeditions, well equipped with modern arms? It seemed impossible; but as he gazed he saw the trenches connecting up the various rivers encircling all the town, and he

was soon forced to confess that the task he had undertaken might prove formidable.

Hardly had the troops encamped when an attack
broke out, the Jagunços having crept up like snakes
amongst the bushes and the grass, without a sign of
their approach. Two companies which had been
thrown out in advance bore the full brunt of the
assault, and suffered heavily. When the moon rose,
about the middle of the night, there was a general
attack upon them. This lasted for an hour or two,
and as the first faint streaks of dawn appeared the
Jagunços silently withdrew, having inflicted heavy
losses on the troops, almost without a casualty to themselves, shooting the soldiers down from the shelter of
the darkness, as they fired wildly, at the flashing of
their guns.

When morning broke at last, the General buried
his dead, and then got his artillery into position,
hoping to end the matter in a day or two with his
superior arms, and to return a victor from the field
where all his predecessors had failed lamentably.
Thus once again, lost in the heart of the Sertão, was
the stage set for the old contest between the forces
representing law and order, and the old world, in
which each man was a law unto himself—the world
of myths and portents, prophets and miracles. The old
and new stood face to face before Canudos, one savage,
brutal, but not the least ashamed; the other painted
in bands of parti-coloured hue, with Progress,
Humanity, and Toleration writ large upon them. On
the one side a pack of wolves, and on the other
a submarine, charged with torpedoes and with mines.

CHAPTER XVI

THOUGH with the force the Government had assembled before Canudos there could be no doubt of their ultimate success, ill luck dogged all their efforts from the start. The fatal habit of holding the Jagunços too cheaply as enemies cost them the lives of many of their best officers and a great toll of casualties amongst their men. On the morning of the 28th the artillery opened fire upon Canudos at the first dawn of day. It was to be expected that the miserably built town would be reduced to ashes in a few hours, under the fire of modern guns.

Events proved that the defenders of the place had natural military instincts of a high order for defence. Hardly had the guns begun to fire, than from pits constructed so as to be invisible, from trenches in the town and from the thick bush, that the imprudent leader of the governmental forces had omitted to destroy, a well-sustained rifle-fire was opened on the artillerymen. In half an hour they had lost more than a hundred men and many officers.

Their fire, to their astonishment, made little impression on the town, except to level open lines through the mud-built houses, the inhabitants all having taken shelter in hiding-places underground. The Jagunço sharp-shooters, led by Pajehú, revealed a courage and a coolness under fire quite unexpected of them by their enemies. Safe in their hiding-places, they lay hid under a hail of projectiles, replying instantly when the storm slackened by a well-directed fire. The General, Arthur Oscar, mad with rage at losing so many of his best men, ordered a general assault. His troops rushed down the hill, entering the town after having forded the little river that had proved so disastrous a passage to the third expedition, and soon were swallowed up in the labyrinth of lanes. A hurricane of fire burst on them from every side ; from houses, trenches, rifle-pits and from the church, they were exposed to a veritable massacre. After having penetrated to the square, destroying street after street of huts as they advanced, in order to secure themselves from an attack in the rear, they were forced to execute what the General described in his despatch as a " well-executed strategic movement, that placed our forces once more under the protection of the guns."

In fact, he had suffered a reverse, and lost, since daybreak, more than three hundred men. The situation was not pleasant. His men were on half rations, and the provision mule-trains had been attacked upon the road by the Jagunços, who, although forced to retire, had wounded many of the pack animals and caused a long delay.

Water was plentiful in the stream that flowed below the spot on which the General was encamped. The passage to and fro to it was rendered possible by the artillery.

Situated as he was, the General's first necessity was to reinforce his troops. Most anxiously he waited for the arrival of General Savaget, whom he had dispatched with a column of two thousand men and several Krupp guns, to converge on the position and take it in the rear.

He too had been attacked upon the road, for the Jagunços displayed much greater enterprise on this occasion than they had done before. At the rate of two leagues* a day, the column under General Savaget toiled through the sand, its marches regulated by the necessity of reaching water and pasture for the animals. It hugged the banks of the River Vasa-Barris, so as to be protected on one flank.

Successively it passed the miserable villages or half-ruined "fazendas" of Passagem, Canna Brava, Brejinho, Manary, Cauché and Serra Vermelha, camping on June the 25th at a place called Cocorobó, where they expected they would be attacked. For the first time a Brazilian General did not fall into the trap laid for him by the Jagunços, with his eyes closed and over-confident.

At this place the only road ran through a deep defile. A cavalry detachment sent on to reconnoitre found the position entrenched and held in force. Nothing remained to General Savaget but to advance and carry the defences with the bayonet. Advancing through a fire that decimated them, the Brazilian infantry displayed the admirable qualities that they have always shown, when they have been well-

* The Brazilian league is about three English miles, rather more than less.

officered and led. On this occasion they sustained their reputation to the full.

Attacked on every side, in a position in which it was impossible to use their superior weapons to advantage, their officers falling like corn before the sickle, under the fire of a concealed and watchful enemy, they steadily advanced. Rocks bounded down the slopes of the defile like greyhounds, making great breaches in their ranks. Their officers fell fast under the fire of hidden sharpshooters. Now and then figures appeared on the high cliffs, fired, and with a yell sank back again under the shelter of a rock. Never before had the Jagunços held a position with such tenacity. It seemed as if for the first time they really comprehended that their country was a natural fortress, with points of vantage arranged by Providence.

The General's horse was killed, and he, when he had disengaged himself from the fallen animal, advanced on foot, followed by the harassed infantry, until at last, with heavy losses, they emerged upon the plain. Thenceforward their progress was a continuous fight. From every rock and tree, or from the midst of the tall grass and bushes, unseen sharpshooters galled their march, taking a heavy toll of them in casualties.

Bands of light horsemen, their leather clothes blending so well with the landscape as to render them almost invisible at a little distance off, picked up the stragglers, lassoing them and trailing them to death behind their horses, in sight of the raging but impotent troops upon the march. The cavalry of the Government, heavily equipped, could never come up

14

to engage the Jagunço horsemen, who fled into the bush, hanging alongside their horses and firing underneath their necks, after the fashion of the Arabs, or the Indians of the plains. Little by little the enemy fell back, disputing every coign of vantage, and when at last the column reached Favella, their losses in the three leagues they had travelled totalled three hundred men.

Once at Favella, General Savaget sent off a messenger to announce his safe arrival to the Commander-in-Chief, only a mile away. The messenger returned with urgent orders to advance. When the tired soldiers arrived outside the main encampment on the farther slopes of Mount Favella, just above the town, they found it invested by the Jagunços on every side. Thus the first task General Savaget found waiting for him was to relieve his own commander and his forces who were blockaded on the hill.

Their greatest need was for provisions, for the Jagunços were holding up the mule trains that had been left inadequately protected on the road. Next day, by a vigorous movement of the two columns, General Savaget was able to free the encampment from the disastrous position it was in, and force the enemy with heavy losses to retire into the town.

The situation was ironical enough. By far the largest and best furnished force the Government had sent against Canudos, owing to fatal over-confidence, found itself virtually besieged, in what should have been a strong position, by the very people it had set out to subdue.

Nine hundred casualties testified to the resistance of the Jagunços to the columns on the march. The

superior arms they had collected from the former
expeditions placed them more on an equality with
the forces of the Government than they had been
before.   Their knowledge of the country, and the
certainty that they all fought with halters round their
necks, made them most formidable antagonists.   In
Pajehú, ex-malefactor and assassin, they had found a
leader of no mean order in the field.   He seems to
have thoroughly comprehended the strength and
weakness of the men he led to the assault, and took
good care never to fall into his previous error of
launching them upon the well-armed troops in the
open, but resorted to the guerilla tactics natural to
every frontierman in every country of the world.

Days passed, during which the soldiers on half
rations, short of water, and confined within a narrow
space, began to murmur at their fate.   The famous
Whitworth gun, that had cost so much intensity of
toil to bring up from the base, was wrongly sighted and
could not be depressed sufficiently to bear upon the
town.   Thus it became a " monstrous fetish,"* but a
fetish without a moral value, as the Jagunços soon
found out its uselessness.   Provisions daily ran lower,
and the chief train of mules, which had left Queimadas nearly a month before, was still held back upon
the road.   The bombardment of the town did not
give the results that were expected of it, and by the
2nd of July the situation of the expedition was
almost desperate.

Their fate depended on provisions, and the pro-

* " Monstruoso fetiche," Euclydes da Cunha, " Os Sertoẽs,"
p. 430.

visions still were delayed upon the road. Men they had plenty of, and ammunition, but not a sack of flour, nor any salt or beans, and beans are the chief staple of the Brazilian troops. Luckily for them, the country to the rear was open to them, and luckier still, a squadron all composed of Gauchos from the south was with the cavalry. These men, centaurs before the Lord, trained to the lazo and the bolas from their youth upwards, proved invaluable. Just as did Garibaldi before Rome, when in a like position to the Brazilian General before Canudos, these Gauchos were sent out to scour the country and drive in all the cattle they could find. Nothing escaped their vigilance, and in a day or two bands of thin cattle were driven in towards the troops. It was a joyful moment when the Gauchos, hurling their long, hide lazos through the air like snakes, planted them unerringly upon the horns of a lean cow or bullock, and dragged it to the ground. In an instant, like a flock of vultures, the soldiers swarmed round the fallen animal, despatched it with their sword bayonets, and speedily put down the joints to roast before the fire. The food put spirit once again into their hearts.

At best it was a temporary expedient, for all the Gauchos could secure were ten or twelve lean animals a day, and that was little when distributed amongst six thousand men, all clamouring for food. The supply of cattle soon was exhausted, and no resource remained but to hunt the goats that had gone wild amongst the hills, and to dig underneath the ground for "as patatas do Vaqueiro,"* a root that has saved

* See Introduction, p. 17.

life, in drought and famine, a thousand times in the Sertão.

Desertions soon became frequent, but ceased when it was known that those who escaped death by thirst and hunger on the road usually fell into the hands of the Jagunços and were killed instantly. No news arrived of the provision train up to the middle of July, and the Commander of the expedition found himself forced either to retreat and face the perils of the march, and the disgrace that he was sure awaited him at home, or else establish communication with the train of mules that he knew must be by this time not far off upon the road. As a last resource he got together such of his cavalry as had horses not too much exhausted for the march, and sent them back to serve as escort to the advancing mule trains, that he awaited with the same feelings as a shipwrecked sailor watching for a sail.

On the 11th of July, when hope was almost dried up in their hearts, and the harassed General was just about to order a retreat, with the first streaks of day-light in the sky, a friendly Sertanejo rode into the camp. Behind him came three troopers mounted on horses, lame and travel-worn. The countryman was the conveyer of a message from the officer in command of the escort that accompanied the train. He had arrived at a day's journey from the encampment, but feared to cross the danger zone with the small forces that he led.

The Sertanejo looked at the starving men with wonder, as he sat like an equestrian statue on his horse, for, in the fashion of his countrymen, he would not alight without a special invitation, as to have done so would have been a breach of courtesy. Slowly he reined his horse back towards where the General and his officers stood waiting for him, making it rear and passage as he went. Taking his hat off, he drew the letter from it, and after handing it to the General, at a sign of welcome, swung himself in one motion from the saddle, and taking off his horse's bridle, he sat down silently to smoke, with his eyes fixed on vacancy, but observing everything.

Joy rang through the encampment, and when at last, next day at evening, long trains of mules laden with bread and flour, with rum, with sugar, coffee, and with jerked beef, filed slowly into the hunger-stricken camp, the soldiers' spirits rose, and they demanded to be led to the attack.

Next day they rested and refreshed themselves. The General held a council with his officers. Night fell upon the camp, amidst a clang of preparations, of songs, of horses neighing, and all the animation that takes hold of men in like positions, who know that it may be the last occasion when they will laugh and sing.

Then, in the starry silence of the tropic night, the *Ave Maria* ascended from the town, and the long melopea of the litanies.

CHAPTER XVII

IT was indeed time for the matter to be decided in one way or another. The concussion of the Government's reverse had been felt to the remotest corner of Brazil. Canudos had become a household word. Right up in Amazonas; in the dark glades of Matto Grosso; on the frontiers of Guiana, the little village in the Sertão of Bahia was known to everyone.

In Rio Grande do Sul, the sceptical and careless Gauchos talked of it at cattle-markings and at fairs, laughing and making game of both sides, after their usual way. The Government, they saw, was weak, and yet they did not give much credence to Antonio Conselheiro's wonder-working powers. After the materialistic fashion of most dwellers upon plains where horses are plentiful, a piece of beef, a cup of maté, a fine day, a handsome girl, or a good horse, engrossed their minds more than the possible destruction of the world, foretold by the prophet of the Sertão. Such clergy as they had amongst them had to ride them on a light hand, or they would have revolted altogether from their control. In the same way the Bedouin Arabs of Arabia, living under conditions so similar to those of the Gauchos on the plains of South America, have always been refractory to religious teaching, holding Islam but at the most a council of perfection, and living, even to-day, much as their forbears lived in the days when the seven poems of the Moalakat were written, and hung up for all men to admire.

Mountains, with mist and ever-changing weather, streams, lakes and waterfalls with rainbows playing on them, great trees, and life circumscribed within more or less narrow limits by the valleys and the hills, drive men to introspection, and to a feeling of their own impotence, before the superior force of Nature. On the wide plains, man is his own star, and the horse places him more on a level with natural forces; not caring to scale a heaven that is not imminent, he is content to live his life, lord of the earth, and, in a greater measure than elsewhere, makes his own destiny.

The dangerous feeling, half of amazement, half of ridicule, that had been excited by the defeats they had incurred, and by the long delay to which their relatively great fourth expedition had been subjected, stirred up the Government, and they sent messages to their Commander not to put off attack.

Upon the other side, and notwithstanding that he must have known the end was certain, Antonio Conselheiro gave no sign of weakness, but set himself resolutely to meet the Government's assault. His past successes had so much increased his fame, that from the eternal forests and swamps of Matto Grosso, from those deep matted woods where giant trees spring up two hundred feet in height, and where the only way to penetrate the thickets is by following the streams,

from every little clearing, recruits once more flocked
to the Sertão.   They came on donkeys and on mules,
on bullocks and on foot, following the forest trails.
For weeks they marched under a tangled vegetation,
so thick that the sun's rays had never penetrated to
the ground.   Humming birds darted to and fro in the
rare clearings, like flakes of topaz or of amethyst.
The pilgrims never heeded them, nor turned their
heads, when now and then in passing over little plains
flocks of macaws—green, red and yellow—soared
past like falcons, uttering their hoarse cry.

Great troops of monkeys gambolled in the woods,
performing their aerial gymnastics as it were for the
travellers' amusement, swinging from tree to tree.   At
night they raised their melancholy chorus, howling
like foghorns, heard dimly through the folds of a sea
mist.   The men and women tramping along were no
more moved with their nocturnal psalmody than with
their feats upon the trees.   With their minds fixed
upon their Zion, Canudos, the mystic city where their
prophet dwelt, for which they had sold all their poor
possessions and set forth to see him and to touch his
raiment, the misguided, but perhaps happy and con-
tented, illuminated folk endured their misery upon
the road.   They passed by back-waters, carpeted over
with the giant leaves of the Victoria Regia, upon
whose banks were egrets, white as snow, standing
immovable, with something sacred in their look, as
they watched for the fish beneath the steaming waters
of the lake.   Across their path, now and then, bounded
wild cats and jaguars, their spotted skins blending
exactly with the prevailing plants and vegetation, so

that in an instant they had become a part of it, and disappeared. From the tall tree tops amongst the purple, red, and multi-coloured flowers of the lianas, came the sloth's melancholy cry. Tapirs and peccaries passed in full view of them, and in the streams they crossed, carpinchos* swam, their heads awash, looking like little hippopotami. Huge logs rolled lazily into the water, showing themselves to have been alligators. Deep in the recesses of the forests, came the sonorous notes of the bell-bird, which makes one think that somewhere there must be a chapel in the woods left by the Jesuits, or else its wraith, served by some phantom priest. All the bright wonders, and the dark melancholy of the tropic everglades, was unrolled before the eyes of these modern Israelites, plodding along towards their stony, burned-up Canaan, guided but by the fiery pillar each one carried in his heart.

When they arrived before the reed-built, palm-thatched city they stopped and broke out into psalmody. All that they had endured was counted nothing, for now they could not err upon the path towards salvation, with Zion full in view.

The rude Paulistas from their cattle farms round Surucába, the miners from Goyáz, the gatherers of caoutchouc in the Amazonian forests, sent their contingents; and from all parts and portions of the mighty empire so many pilgrims came that they were forced to encamp, and build great villages of huts.

"See Rome and lose your faith," † the adage ran in

* The Capybara of naturalists. The largest known member of the rodent family.

† "Roma veduta, fede perduta."

the old days, when the spiritual descendant of the Galilean fishermen used to dominate the world. Whether Canudos, ill-built and dirty, poor and miserable, with its sectarian life of sexual licence and eternal psalmody, had a like effect upon the pilgrims, is known to no man.   After the catastrophe, most of them disappeared again into the forest trails from which they had emerged, and by degrees regained their homes, leaving as little traces of their passage as does a flight of flying fish after its brief excursion into air.

Within the town, the spiritual life daily became more highly keyed up, and still more intense.   The prophet passed the day in preparations for defence ; the night in prayer and preaching, and all the sectaries under his ministrations prepared themselves to die.   As often happens in like circumstances, either in times of pestilence or siege, the people all abandoned themselves to sexual excesses, only to be paralleled amongst their prototypes in Phrygia and in Cilicia, when the contending Orthodox and Gnostic sects strove for the mastery.   " God's people ever were a backsliding folk," ran the old Scottish saying, and the same proved true in the Sertão.   This did not stop them from laying plans for their defence with judgment and with skill.   Thus fortified, both by their trenches and their faith, they stood at bay, awaiting the last move of the Government.

They had not long to wait, for on the 18th of July, after his troops had rested and reinforcements had come up, General Arthur Oscar gave the signal for attack.   For the last day or two the artillery had rained shells upon the town, but their effect was inconsiderable. Either the artillerymen were not trained to their task, or the fragile nature of the houses of the town allowed the projectiles to pass through them like paper, without exploding, or for some other cause, the bombardment failed of its result. Nothing was left but an assault in force, and this was fixed for the 18th of July. As usual, the spirits of the troops ran high. All were most anxious to be led to the attack, and once again they fell into the trap of over-confidence. It seemed impossible that six thousand well-armed men, furnished with ample ammunition and artillery, should not at once possess themselves of a miserable town of shanties, defended by men void of discipline. Civilised and disciplined soldiers are always at their worst and weakest in wild countries. All is unfamiliar to them. They see no houses, churches, cows, or sheep and horses grazing ; there are no hedges, ditches, railway embankments, or any of the familiar features of a European landscape. Distances are always greater than those they have been used to in their homes. The atmosphere is puzzling, crows appear bullocks, bullocks crows, in the clear air. A range of hills that looks a few miles distant may prove a long day's journey off. Insensibly, the confidence of the training camp is undermined, for the enemy they have been taught to expect under conditions not unlike their own is never visible, and on the rare occasions when he shows himself seems like a phantom of the night. Then, when the troops begin to think he is contemptible, and that their task will prove a military promenade, a feeling that invariably overtakes disciplined, well-armed men in such surroundings, without a moment's warning, out of nothing as it were, up from the long grass, behind a line of stones, or from the reeds upon a river's bank, the long-sought enemy appears, and in an instant inflicts considerable loss. Fury possesses every heart, that men they had despised could prove so formidable, and fury turns to impotency when the troops find, encumbered as they are with all the lumber of a European regiment, that all pursuit is vain.

Such warfare tries the best of troops to the utmost, as we found in South Africa, and as the French found in the Soudan. In the Sertão it was intensified, for the men the army was opposed to were their own countrymen. The soldiers passed the night in celebrating the expected victory. At daybreak they moved to the attack, advancing bravely under the fire of their artillery and entering the town. As upon former instances, not a shot was fired by the Jagunços until the soldiers were well engaged amongst the streets, and the artillery was obliged to cease its fire, for fear of killing their own soldiers with the enemy. When the long columns of the troops had entered the tortuous lanes of huts, the fire of the Jagunços broke out upon them. This time the sectaries were better armed—with the rifles and the ammunition they had taken from the former expeditions—and the troops, huddled up amongst the lanes, soon suffered terribly. Men fell on all sides, but the attack was well sustained, and did not lose its energy till it had carried a little eminence that looked down on the interior of the town. Had there been forces in sufficient numbers to advance, well officered and led, the fate of Canudos would shortly have been sealed ; but nearly all the officers had fallen, and the attacking column was completely isolated. The General rushed up reinforcements, and the position was assured ; but the troops who had fought bravely all through the day were thoroughly worn out.

Camped on the eminence that they had conquered, but unable to go on, the new encampment found itself isolated, with its advance into the town rendered impossible, and its communications with the base dangerous and difficult. The night passed unmolested, and they employed it in digging trenches and in strengthening the hill. When morning broke they were surrounded by the enemy, and from the huts issued a swarm of women and girls, all armed with hatchets and with knives, butchering the wounded as they lay helpless on the ground. Three times the General-in-Chief rushed reinforcements up to them, only to see them beaten back again. Then, getting off his horse, he headed the fourth charge in person, advancing bravely through a storm of bullets, till he reached the eminence. After a council, he determined to hold on at any cost, and to take the town, street after street, or house by house, if it proved necessary.

Dreams of a swift triumph now had vanished, and all the officers perceived that it would take a siege extending over months to make an end of it. A thousand casualties in the last operation had considerably reduced his forces, and the General, though much against his will, was forced to ask for reinforcements once again for his depleted ranks.

The next few days passed quietly, for on both sides the casualties had been enormous, so for the moment the days were passed in skirmishing, in which the troops lost heavily in their exposed positions ; and the enemy, if he lost many men, was always able to conceal his losses and carry off his dead.

All day the noise of firing went on ceaselessly, and then at nightfall, whilst the troops sat silent round their fires, the sound of litanies was wafted from the town, as if the inhabitants looked on the fighting as a mere incident, and when the darkness fell upon their town, turned to reality.

CHAPTER XVIII

Wʜɪʟsᴛ General Arthur Oscar waited for reinforcements after having sent his wounded back to the railhead, a journey that they had to do on foot, on mules, in bullock carts, almost without provisions and exposed to sun and rain, the partisans of Antonio Conselheiro grew more daring every day. Not content with blockading the advanced section of their invaders closely in their camp, they raided all the country for miles on every side. They took the town of Viela de Santa Anna and sacked it utterly, and wasted the whole district of Mirandella, burning the houses and carrying the cattle off from all the farms. With their instinctive eye for strategical position they fortified a post upon the hills near Varzea da Ema, and another at Caypán. As these points dominated the chief road from Monte Santo, all the trains of ammunition and of provisions coming to the camp were constantly attacked. Nothing could pass along the road without an escort, and even then mule train and escort were often beaten back and forced to wait for reinforcements on the way.

Under the impulse of fanaticism, with a contempt of death equal to that shown by the tribes of the Soudan, old Macambira's son, with ten or twelve companions, planned to carry off the big gun, which, now that it had been put into working order, did great execution on the town. Creeping like snakes through the long grass and using every artifice of frontier warfare to conceal their progress, they crawled into the camp. The men were sleeping, and the sentinels did not perceive them, till they rose silently, like phantoms, close beside the gun. If heroism be a contempt of death, the devoted twelve who followed Macambira were heroes verily, for death was certain in their enterprise.

Hardly had the gun begun to move under their united efforts than the alarm was raised. Alone amongst six thousand men, they all fell dead around their prize, except one man, who in a hail of bullets, brandishing his knife as he ran, leaping from side to side, reached some bushes into which he disappeared, just as a fish is lost to view after it leaps and falls back in the stream.

Troops were converging on Canudos from every point of the republic of Brazil. So serious did the situation seem to Ministers that they sent their Secretary of State for War, Marshal de Bittencourt, to take the chief command. This officer was cast in a different mould from all his predecessors. Cold, calculating, and never to be moved from the goal he had in view, his first care was to collect an overwhelming force.

In a short time nearly ten thousand men, with a whole park of artillery, were brought together, and converged upon the place. Marshal de Bittencourt had no idea of leaving anything to chance, nor did he suffer from the over-confidence into which the other generals had fallen.   By the middle of September all was ready at the railhead for an advance in force.

The short season of the summer was over, and already the Sertão was putting on an aspect of drought and of aridity, with scarcity of pasture, long days of heat and nights of frost—a season most unfavourable to troops, but advantageous to the last degree to the Jagunços, to whom the weather, heat, cold, thirst, or hunger were indifferent.

Moreover, the position in General Arthur Oscar's camp was most precarious. Inaction, with the scarcity of food, had brought on frequent desertions, and the deserters, who dared not face the perils of the road, remained in bands, hanging about the woods and issuing forth, when they were strong enough, to attack provision trains.

The Jagunços, who seemed to have ample supplies of ammunition, perpetually attacked the camp and cut off stragglers, and day by day, by hunger, battle, and disease, the General's forces dwindled until all that he could do was to remain on the defensive in his camp—to such a pass had the Jagunços, helped by their climate and the want of roads, reduced a force of full six thousand soldiers, armed and disciplined, and backed by modern guns.   The monstrous, incompleted temple, that the fire of the artillery had failed to batter down, still dominated the camp of the besieging force. The Jagunços had erected crows' nests on it, from which they spied each movement in the camp, and from its highest points sharp-shooters were ensconced, that could not be dislodged by the artillery fire.

Inside the town enthusiasm ran high. The ignorant Jagunços had no idea of the strength of the two contending parties, and even if they had, looked to a miracle from their good Councillor that would redeem their town. What men such as were Pajehú and Macambira, Joao Abade, and the rest of the guerilla leaders thought, no one can tell, but it may be such worldly wisdom as they had was swallowed up in the general wave of superstition prevailing in the town. None of them faltered, and not one of them attempted to escape what they must all have known was the impending doom, but fought on faithfully, giving their lives as cheerfully as did the rudest and most uneducated.

No prisoners had been taken, for the Jagunços gave no quarter, and on their own side carried off all their wounded, so that neither party had the least knowledge of its opponent's mind. So serious the situation had become by the end of September that, had not Marshal de Bittencourt been already on the road, the fourth expedition would have been forced to straggle back to Monte Santo after the fashion of its predecessors. General Barbosa, the second in command, had been dangerously wounded, right in the middle of the camp, and every regiment was depleted by a third of its full strength by desertion and disease, and by the losses of the fight. The Marshal's force was now upon the road, advancing steadily, as if it had been in a foreign country rather than in Brazil, with scouts thrown out on every side, and searching all the bushes with artillery.

When it arrived it found the troops of General

Arthur Oscar almost at the last gasp for want of food and every necessary. A day or two put all in order, and with ten thousand men, provisions, guns, ammunition, and reinforcements pouring in from every side, the fate of the Jagunço Zion was settled, although it still held out. As time passed by, little by little the troops advanced, inexorably destroying all the houses as they went, so as not to leave defences in the rear. For the first time some prisoners were taken; but they turned out to be composed of women, of children, and old men past fighting, who had left the town, pushed by the want of food. As they filed past the soldiers, a thrill of pity ran through the ranks, for the prisoners seemed a band of living skeletons. Throughout the past three months of fighting they had starved, and now could hardly drag themselves along. Women who had been fierce viragoes tottered on their feet, leaning on sticks, and miserable mothers pressed their starving infants to their dried up breasts, as they passed like a drove of phantoms through the camp. Three or four boys, of ten or twelve years of age, wounded and black with powder—for they had fought beside their fathers—drew themselves up, and tried to swagger as they saw the soldiers looking at them. The spectral procession gave an indication of what was passing in the town.

Still it gave not a sign of weakness, and every evening the sound of litanies and hymns floated up to the camp, where round the fires, for the first time, the soldiers, amply fed and cared for, listened with feelings of amazement to the psalmody that rose from the doomed town.

September opened disastrously for the besieged. At the beginning of the month Pajehú fell, pierced by a chance shot. His death deprived the sectaries of their most energetic leader, and the command devolved on Macambira and João Abade, who carried on the fight to the best of their ability, but with less genius for guerilla warfare than Pajehú had shown. Early in the month the two half-finished towers of the great church were battered down, depriving the besieged of their best observation posts, for they had towered above the camp.

Antonio Conselheiro, who had rarely left the towers for weeks, except when he came down to animate his followers, was nearly overwhelmed in the fall of the towers, but once again escaped. His escape was set down to a miracle, and his brave, if misguided, followers still determined to hold out. Inside the town the battle was continuous, for the trenches ran under the houses like a rabbit warren, and when a group of huts had been destroyed, the troops who thought themselves secure found they were exposed to a hot fire from men well hidden underground, and sheltered from attack.

On neither side was quarter given, and the troops instantly cut the throats or ripped the bellies up of every prisoner, knowing the one thing the Jagunços feared was death by steel, thinking it deprived them of salvation—a superstition never yet explained. Thus when the soldiers took a prisoner they asked him generally, " How do you want to die ?"

The Jagunços always answered, " By a rifle shot." Then with a savage laugh the soldiers' answer was,

" It shall be by cold steel," and plunged his knife into his throat, bending the head back as a butcher treats a sheep.

Each lane and every house had to be taken separately, and women, children, and old men fought by the side of the Jagunços, giving their lives as cheerfully as the most robust of the young. Terrible combats took place underground in the rough trenches and in the huts, into which the inhabitants inveigled soldiers, by counterfeiting death and then attacking them. Whichever side carried the day in these encounters, the fate of those defeated was assured, and the long " jacaré " of the Jagunços, or the sword-bayonet of the troops, was the sole arbiter.

To all the propositions of surrender made by the Marshal no answer was returned. The prisoners refused to answer questions as to the condition of the town, even to save their lives. After refusal they were slain inexorably ; but young and old alike refused their lives, saying they wished to follow their good Councillor to heaven, of which they were assured.

Once more the besiegers tried a general assault, furious to be delayed too long by such a miserable place. It failed completely, under the terrific fire that burst upon it from huts and trenches, churches, and from the four Krupp guns, lost by the former expedition, after its defeat. Furious, the Marshal led his forces back again, and once again sat down to draw the investment tighter and to prevent provisions from arriving at the town.

One gate of safety still remained to the stubborn sectaries. The roads towards Varzea da Ema and

Uauá still were open to them.   Provisions still came
in occasionally, and a supply of ammunition reached
them, sent by traders on the coast, following the
forest trails.   By these, the population could have
escaped to the interior, or at the least the leaders and
the able-bodied men.   Behind them was immunity, for
the Government could not have followed them into
the trackless wilds of Matto Grosso.   Behind them
lay relief from hunger, safety from danger, and the
possibility of founding a new Zion remote from inter-
ference, where they could have lived and looked for
the coming of the King, Don Sebastian, and followed
their peculiar doctrines in peace.   So hard the
Government was pushed, even with the larger forces
under Marshal Bittencourt, that probably they would
have been willing to come to a composition of some
sort or other with Antonio Conselheiro, had he but
made a sign.   Neither he nor his stubborn followers
gave the sign, and what is more remarkable, none of
the bandits, thieves, or broken men who could not be
supposed to have joined him for religious motives,
ever thought of an escape.   Provisions for a time
came in by the two open roads, and a few old 'men
and women with their children disappeared along
them, into the forest wilds.

By the middle of September, Marshal Bittencourt
advanced and occupied both roads.   Then he sent
in to see if Antonio Conselheiro would surrender,
being well aware that there was still hard work before
him if he should have to reduce the place by force.
No answer was returned to any of his messages, and
the agony of the Jagunço Zion entered its last phase.

Once more the fighting recommenced. The troops advanced, enduring heavy losses, but always gaining ground. Men fought to the last gasp, in trenches, in the dark lanes and winding passages. None asked for quarter, and if a prisoner was taken on either side, he was straightway butchered like a sheep. The wounded were slaughtered as they lay, by starving women who crept out under fire to drive a knife into the victim's heart, content to be shot down, so that, as some of them exclaimed, " I have dispatched a dog before me, to prepare the way." The month crept on, and still Canudos fought with the courage of despair. At last the walls of the great church were battered down, depriving the Jagunços of their battery, for on the church the captured guns had been set up.

The inhabitants, with true Indian stoicism, hungry and desperate, and with ammunition running short, kept on the unequal combat, fighting as desperately as upon the first day they were attacked. Nothing compelled them, for neither Antonio Conselheiro nor his leaders had any special bodies of armed men on whom they could rely, nor, given the character of the Brazilian, they probably would not have applied compulsion if they had had the power.

Hunger began to do its work, and night by night miserable bands of women, their heads enveloped in their white blankets, crept into the besiegers' camp to seek a little food. They said no word, they made no prayer ; but sitting down upon the ground with their heads covered, patiently waited for whatever fate they had to bear. Their appearance sent a thrill of pity through the troops, who shared their rations with them, and then advanced to the attack.

One by one, all the chief leaders disappeared, slain in the trenches, butchered in the lanes, or dead of hunger and of thirst. Last of all, on the 22nd of the month, Antonio Conselheiro died.

As he had seen his hopes all vanish one by one—the great, new town which was to be the centre of the kingdom of Don Sebastian battered to pieces and the walls levelled with the ground, the towers fallen down, the sacred image of the Good Jesus blown to pieces by a shell, his people starving and every hope deceived—he fell into despair. Wrapping himself in silence, he refused all food, passed all the day in prayer in an angle of the ruined church before an image of a saint, and stalked about the streets occasionally, a living skeleton shrouded in mutism.

One day, after he had been missed for several hours, Antonio Beatinho, his inseparable friend and devotee, found him face downwards on the ground, dead and already cold, clasping a silver crucifix against his breast, within the ruined church. His face was calm, his body almost mere skin and bones, worn out with fasting and with the death of his illusions, but his soul unconquerable.

CHAPTER XIX

ANTONIO CONSELHEIRO's death had the effect of
rendering his followers still more desperate and determined to hold out. A legend soon gained ground,
that as he saw his chief adherents and the best part
of all his fighting men slain by the enemy, he had
determined to accompany them as an ambassador to
God. He had died, they said, to expiate their crimes,
and now was sitting at the right hand of God, direct-
ing the defence. Soon, it was rumoured, he would
return in glory, accompanied by the King, Don
Sebastian, and with an escort of angels and arch-
angels, all armed with flaming swords, to fight with
Anti-Christ.

All hearts were lightened, and in spite of hunger
and of thirst the decimated sectaries fought on
stubbornly. A few deserted, and thus saved
themselves, seeking a refuge in the impenetrable
forests, after the hue and cry was over returning to
their houses, where some of them possibly still are
living, waiting for the millennium and for the prophet's
second coming upon earth. Let them live on, and
watch the humming-birds as they hang poised above
the flowers, the lizards basking in the sun, listen to

the mysterious noises that at night in the tropics rise
from the woods, inhale the scent of the dank vegetation, and till their crops of mandioca and of maize.
That is the true millennium, did they but know it, and
each man makes or mars it for himself, as long as
health gives him the power to drink it in, and to
enjoy.

These were the last to escape from the impending
doom, for in October the investment lines were drawn
so strictly that not a mouse could issue from the town.
From that time the doom of the besieged was sealed,
and their destruction certain, if they continued to
resist.   It would have been good policy to have proclaimed an amnesty, for as Antonio Conselheiro and
their other leaders all were dead, the people would
have gone back to their homes had they but only
been assured of safety for their lives.   Few
Governments are much disposed either to pity or to
common sense, and the Brazilians were no exception to
the rule that seems to make republics and monarchies
alike hating and hateful to mankind.

So once again the struggle was begun, with varying
fortunes all through October, and bitterness pushed to
the verge of madness upon both sides reigned indis-
criminately.   Prisoners were taken and dragged before
the General, interrogated, wrapped themselves up in
silence, or defied him, and in both cases by a motion
of the hand were sent out to their death.

Not one of them faltered or weakened for a moment, some of them feeling the edges of the knives
that were next moment to be plunged into their

throats, with a defiant smile. The troops grew weary of the butchery, but there was no respite, and to all offers of surrender no answer was returned.

Water began to fail, and the besieged Jagunços suffered terribly from thirst. To get at water for their comrades and their wives, some performed prodigious acts of bravery, creeping out under fire to fill a miserable skin or gourd, at the utmost hazard of their lives.

As each successive group of huts was taken and destroyed, the next resisted still more stubbornly, taking a heavy toll of killed and wounded from the soldiery. At times, the hunger-driven people, collecting all the men fit to bear arms, charged desperately upon the troops, amongst whose files a feeling of commiseration grew for their mad valour and their contempt of death. All night the artillery played upon the town, lighting it up as the shells set the miserable huts afire, and battering down such portions of the church as still were standing, destroying the last points of vantage for the sharp-shooters.

Nothing could break the resolution of the fast disappearing sectaries, and when the roaring of the guns was stilled, the long-drawn notes of psalms were wafted through the night, but now more fitfully, like the lost souls in purgatory, raising a cry for help.

To the repeated messages sent by the Marshal for surrender still no answer was returned, even an offer of an armistice was only used by the Jagunços to send out a crowd of starving women, who, headed by Antonio Beatinho, defiled like phantoms through the camp, victims for months of hunger and thirst.   The fighting men retired still deeper into the dark recesses of the lanes, and kept up a hot fire upon the troops with their last cartridges.

Days passed, days which must have been weeks to the pent-up defenders of the town, cooped in their trenches and their rifle-pits.   Throughout October the miserable butchery dragged on, until at last, on the 5th of November, 1897, all was as silent as the grave.   No shots were fired from the smoking heaps of ruins, and not a hymn was raised by the Jagunços to their lost Councillor.   The soldiers, fearing an ambuscade, advanced, passing by trenches filled to the top with dead, and through the lanes, strewn thick with corpses lying as they fell, some at the door of their own huts, and others with their faces in the mud-holes towards which they had crept to seek a little water in their agony.

All the Jagunços had joined their Councillor.   From the last trench the soldiers received the fire of the few last defenders of Canudos, faithful to the death.   Two boys, one able-bodied man, and an old veteran, still fought on until a volley from the soldiers laid them at rest, their faces turned towards the foe.

Under a covering of earth, in a grave, shallow, and dug in haste, the conquerers, after a search, came on the body of Antonio Conselheiro.   Dressed in his long, blue tunic, his hands crossed piously, clasping a crucifix against his breast, he lay, waiting the coming of the King, that Don Sebastian who he believed should come to rule the world in glory, blot out injustice, cast down the mighty, and exalt the poor in spirit, giving them the earth as their inheritance.

Some of the faithful had placed some withered flowers upon his breast. His body lay upon a ragged piece of matting, and both his eyes were full of sand.

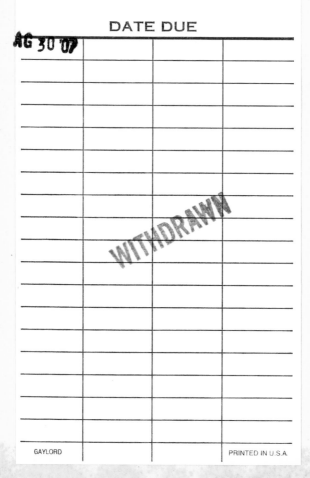